NEW HORIZONS
FOR THE
THIRD WORLD

By Francisco Casanova Alvarez

FOREWORD BY SOL M. LINOWITZ, CHAIRMAN OF THE
COMMISSION ON U.S. - LATIN AMERICAN RELATIONS

PUBLIC AFFAIRS PRESS, WASHINGTON, D. C.

The author is indebted to Mario Rosales Betancourt, Maricela
Daniel Velasco, and Francisco Lopez Valadez for their collabo-
ration in researching and organizing much of the background
material for this book. He is also grateful to Rebecca Garcia
Ortega and Silvia Garcia Andrade for secretarial assistance.
Translation and editorial assistance was provided by Thalia
Terrell, Larry Hanlon, Glen Reitze, and Rolfe W. Larson.

FOREWORD

The Irish poet, Arthur O'Shaughnessy, once wrote: "Each age is a dream that is dying or one that is coming to birth". The age that is coming to birth—indeed, the one that is already upon us—is so changing and dynamic that no one can really know how it will be to live in it. We can be sure, however, that the habits of the past will not be sufficient to meet the challenges of the future.

Today we have come to recognize our true interdependence in this global environment and to understand that there are other important centers of power in the world besides the superpowers. We know that transnational forces, including the multinational corporation, have become important factors on the international scene. We know also that when we think of security we can no longer think of military and political power alone, but must also think of oil and copper and bauxite. We must think of the implications of the urgent prospect of world famine due to the scarcity of food and fertilizer. We must think of the impact of the population problem—of the fact that 4 billion people now dwell on this earth; by the turn of the century there will be 8 billion or more.

If one thing has become clear it is that we must realistically confront the terrible disparity in living conditions between the so-called developed North and the underdeveloped South—between the world's "haves" and "have-nots"—a gap which has been described as the most tragic and urgent problem of our day. The tragedy is in the economic despair and emptiness that mark the lives of all too many in the developing countries; the urgency is in preventing a political reaction that could damage international peace and security.

For we simply cannot expect to live peacefully in a world more than half enslaved by poverty, with only the minority free from want and fear of want. There can be no security for anyone in a world of injustice and resentment, a world in which the future balance of power will ultimately be decided by men and nations now lumped under the misleading label "underdeveloped."

Certainly today there no longer exists—if, indeed, there ever did exist—any meaningful demarcation between the world's economic and political problems. To categorize an issue as economic does not minimize its political ramifications. Coffee, sugar and cocoa may be breakfast foods in the United States, but in Latin America and in Africa they are the stuff revolutions feed upon.

It is against this backdrop that this book must be read and appraised. For it is an effort to present clearly and thoughtfully the factors which led to the Charter of Economic Rights and Duties of States approved by the United Nations General Assembly on December 12, 1974. The Charter represents the response of the developing world to some of the deep-seated problems that have been accumulating over the years and sets forth the hopes and aspirations of these nations as they view the future. As such, the Charter deserves the careful study and analysis which it receives in the book—not only for what it says, but for the circumstances which led to its promulgation.

There may be some reason to question various aspects of the Charter and whether various of the prescriptions will, indeed, meet the needs. But none can quarrel with the seriousness of purpose and conviction which moved the nations to endorse the Charter as reflective of their deep concerns.

As the book makes abundantly clear, the Charter owes its origin to President Luis Echeverria of Mexico, who was the Charter's proponent and became the mainspring behind its adoption. President Echeverria took upon himself the mission of trying to crystalize on behalf of the developing countries this aggregation of economic rights and duties. In doing so he was drawing upon his own deep concern, knowledge and experience, which won the respect and support of the countries which endorsed the Charter.

In taking the leadership to put forward a document which challenges early assumptions and re-examines and re-evaluates the international course for the future, President Echeverria, on behalf of his country, made a singular and lasting contribution.

SOL M. LINOWITZ

CONTENTS

1: From the Bipolar
to the Polycentric World

The crisis of the postwar world encompasses many economic, political, sociological, and ideological aspects. Its depth and scope may be understood only through a consideration of all these factors and their close interrelationships. None of them is independent; each is to some extent both a cause and consequence of the others. This is not to say that there is a "cause-and-effect" relationship in a unidirectional sense, but rather that there is an interaction among the factors which cumulatively have produced and aggravated present-day problems.

World War II was above all a conflict that involved virtually all of the industrialized countries. In 1939 the industrial world consisted primarily of the United States, Canada, England, the Soviet Union, Germany, Belgium, France, Italy, Norway, Austria, Czechoslovakia, the Netherlands, and Japan as well as Sweden and Switzerland. With the exception of the last two, all of these countries participated directly in the war, and each participant except the United States and Canada suffered considerable damage to its industrial base.

The economic effects of the war, especially in the nations that were the epicenter of the catastrophe, nearly resulted in the disappearance of European civilization. For this reason, when the war ended, it was considered imperative to reconstruct Europe rapidly. Such conviction arose both from humanitarian sentiment and nostalgic concern for "the cradle of Western civilization", as well as from fear that economic and social unrest would precipitate political upheavals. Therefore, in 1947 the Marshall Plan was devised by the United States for the specific purpose of rebuilding Europe's industrial structure.

From the viewpoint of the industrial countries, the Marshall Plan was a complete success politically and economically. For the European countries, as well as for Japan, Australia, and the United States, the years that followed the war were a period of exceptional economic growth during which unemployment was nearly eliminated and international trade greatly improved.

On the other hand, the developing nations were left to operate within the narrow margin permitted by the reconstruction of the industrial countries. Some of the underdeveloped nations took advantage of wartime challenges by adopting policies aimed at substitution of domestic products for imports. Others struggled to free themselves from the grip of European colonialism. Unlike the industrial nations, however, the underdeveloped countries lacked the requisite infrastructure for substantial progress. As the economically expanding industrial nations flooded the world's market with an excess of goods, the underdeveloped countries found it difficult to become more self-sufficient under exceedingly disadvantageous circumstances. In addition, large-scale advertising campaigns of the industrial countries created artificial needs in the consumer sector of the underdeveloped nations, thereby further aggravating their problems. By exchanging raw materials for manufactured goods (some of which were luxury items), the underdeveloped nations exchanged their colonial dependency for imperialistic economic dependency.

Moreover, improvements in health care and advances in technical and medical knowledge greatly reduced mortality rates among the peoples of developing countries. This resulted in excessive population growth as well as increased pressures and demands on governments hard put to cope with their normal problems.

The monopolistic trends of many large companies—which were seldom restrained by the laws of their home countries and which benefited by arbitrarily fixed prices on the goods they both bought and sold—further complicated international relations for the developing nations.

A direct result of this situation was greater widening of the gap between the developed and underdeveloped nations. Some of these countries substantially enlarged their industrial and financial potential; others suffered economically and became more dependent. While the wealth of some nations rose rapidly, the misery of others increased proportionately. On a strictly national level, class stratification, internal differences and conflicts within the developing nations were exacerbated by economic dependence on industrial countries. These conditions, in turn, made it extremely difficult to resolve fundamental problems and take concerted action on domestic development projects.

In the Yalta conference at the end of the war a new balance of power was forged: the world became divided into two main spheres of influence—one ruled by the United States, the other by the Soviet Union. What was left fell to England and France. It was also at Yalta that the ground was laid for the cold war.

The cold war was the ideological veneer of a bipolar international system and of a growing bipolar economic imperialism. Indeed, the ideological Manichaeanism of this war, with its worldwide anti-communist and anti-capitalist crusades supported by the two centers of power—one in the East, the other in the West—distracted attention from the realization that two empires were seeking to dominate the globe.

The military supremacy of the United States and the Soviet Union over the rest of the world was initially solidified by their monopoly of atomic weapons. Their economic power was ensured by their resources, and their technological and scientific know-how. Moreover, their control over international trade was facilitated by their enormous productivity and the volume of their financial resources. In short, the cold war provided the U. S. and Soviet Russia with an ideological disguise for economic and political realities on which their imperialism is based.

The resulting balance of power situation was exceedingly precarious. It depended upon each party respecting the "rules of the international game" they controlled and maintaining the conditions that had given rise to it. This does not, of course, mean that these rules were not violated, nor that international relations remained unchanged. It means that the violations were not grave enough to warrant a serious disruption of the balance of power (not even the Cuban missile crisis, serious as it was, warranted this), or that the balance of power was quickly restored by one of the contenders meddling in the sphere of influence of the original intruder. Within these parameters of coexistence there was a prolonged period of international peace, reconstruction, and economic expansion among the world's industrial nations.

The bipolar balance of power began to break down during the 1960s when serious rifts disrupted the dominant imperialistic systems. The most significant was caused by the birth of new nations following the strains of separation from the mother country. For all practical purposes, the Westminster Statute of 1931 had laid the groundwork for the gradual transformation of the British Empire into a Commonwealth. Indeed, even prior to World War II, Egypt had become independent, but decolonization was a slow, if inexorable, process.

After the war—and as a consequence of it—nations were achieving independence at a rapid rate. During the war, India insisted upon and became entitled to independence. In the postwar period India and China were expected to assume an influential role in international affairs, and it was generally believed that the liberation of the Dutch East Indies was only a matter of time. All in all, decolonization accelerated much more rapidly than could have been imagined when the war ended. By the 1950's decolonization had resulted in marked changes in the political map of the world, especially in the nations of Asia and Africa which had achieved their sovereignty.

After emerging from colonial exploitation (though many were still saddled with tribal structures and serious problems of unity and national identity) some of the new nations recognized that they had to raise the standard of living of their people through economic and social development. Today this recognition has become a Third World ideology—the ideology of development—which has replaced the cold war obsessions. In developing nations the terms "communism" and "capitalism" simply do not have the same meaning as in their countries of origin. The ideological positions of the latter are viewed with much skepticism. Today, in the midst of growing difficulties, the developing nations are insisting upon control of their own destinies without constraint, direct or indirect, by industrial powers.

The differences that exist among the developing countries are great, even among countries with similar cultures in the same geographic area. The same applies to their potential for self-development. All of them, however, share similar goals for development and have the same concern about their disadvantageous positions vis-a-vis the powerful nations. Above all, their poverty unites them because they realize that the wealth available to the industrial nations is directly related to their own poverty; they are poor because the other countries are rich, and vice versa.

At the time of the first United Nations Conference on Trade and Development (UNCTAD) a block of developing nations was formed. Due to its initial number of members, this bloc became known as the "Group of 77". Today this vital new force in international affairs is known as "The Third World".

A conflict between poor and rich nations was thus added to the polarization between the socialist and capitalist blocs. The world is now divided into two groups—"countries that cannot sleep" and "countries that cannot eat".

Because of the proliferation of atomic weapons in recent years, the United States and the Soviet Union no longer have a nuclear monopoly. The fact that other nations have access to nuclear capabilities virtually guarantees that any atomic aggression would trigger some atomic response. For this reason such weapons have lost most of their effectiveness as instruments of dissuasion and pressure. Since the nuclear monopoly has been broken, countries that now possess these weapons have correspondingly increased their bargaining leverage.

Whereas the crack in the postwar world order created by the emergence of new nations and the expansion in the number of nuclear nations have had serious repercussions in the last decade, the fissures within the bipolar power system that have appeared during the same period are no less serious. The denunciation of the Warsaw Pact and subsequent estrangement of several socialist countries (notably Yugoslavia, Rumania, and Czechoslovakia) as well as the final rupture between the Soviet Union and China represent what some scholars call the rise of the middle powers. Clamors for independence have also appeared within the western industrial bloc, which is evident, for example, in the independence with which France has handled her international affairs in recent years.

Moreover, the conflicts between the predominant powers and the middle nations have been aggravated by an accelerated inflationary process and a persistent worldwide monetary crisis, both of which have been exacerbated by the energy crisis. This set of problems is sharpened by an unprecedented population explosion, growing deterioration of the environment, and a scarcity of food throughout large areas of the world. This is the basic context of the current crisis in the world order. One obvious conclusion is inescapable: we are today witnessing a transition in the political structure of the world from a bipolar to a polycentric international system.

2: The Consequences
of Economic Polarization

The present inflationary crisis is due largely to the international monetary system established by the Allied nations at the Bretton Woods Conference of 1944. A subject of considerable debate at the conference was the negative effect, between the World Wars, of economic practices by which some countries prospered at the expense of others through measures which reaped enormous profits from artificial trade advantages.

One of the mechanisms most frequently used by the more developed countries during the 1930's was the simple device of officially devaluating the local currency vis-a-vis foreign currencies. Importers then found themselves paying higher prices for goods they obtained from abroad since their own currency was reduced in value compared with those of exporting countries. The result was a reduction in the volume of imports. On the other hand, foreign currency obtained by local exporters was worth more than formerly in the devalued local currency. Thus imports were discouraged and exports were encouraged. But some countries reacted by devaluating their own currency and some reduced their imports by imposing higher tariffs. The cumulative effect was disastrous for international trade: massive unemployment and economic stagnation spread swiftly from one country to another.

Stimulation of trade and rapid transfer of capital were essential in the monumental task of economic reconstruction of the industrial World War II belligerents. This necessitated an international agreement with respect to exchange rates for the world's currencies—that is, the number of units of any one currency required to purchase a single unit of any other. It was primarily for this purpose that the Allies met in Bretton Woods to establish the two institutions that would sit at the apex of the postwar economic order: the International Monetary Fund and the World Bank.

The World Bank was entrusted with expediting the flow of capital and international investment; the International Monetary Fund was intended to bring into existence a system of viable relationships between national currencies.

The monetary system thus instituted—known as the Bretton Woods system—was based on the so-called "gold exchange standard". Under this standard the reserves of all countries were in gold bullion and some key currencies that could be automatically converted into gold at a fixed price. The United States dollar and the pound sterling became such currencies, and a price was set at $35 an ounce for gold. Parity of currencies of the other signatory countries was established with respect to gold and their rates of exchange were determined with respect to the dollar. In this manner all the currencies became interrelated, with the result that variations in the value of any one of them materially affected the overall system. In order to prevent such tendencies it was decided that only variations of up to 1% above or below the exchange rate would be allowed. The exchange rates could only be modified in the event that a "fundamental imbalance" came about in the balance of payments of the country desiring the change in parity, and only after discussions with the other members of the International Monetary Fund had taken place.

Each member state contributed to the Fund according to its economic capacity. One-fourth of each country's contribution was paid in gold bullion and the remainder in local currency. Voting power within the Fund was keyed precisely to the amount of each member's contribution; this automatically gave predominance to the industrial countries. While the United States contributed 2.7 billion dollars, and England 1.3 billion of a total fund of 8.8 billion dollars, the total amount contributed by all developing countries barely reached 1.9 billion. Therefore, despite their numerical majority, comprising two-thirds of the initial forty-five members, the developing countries were a decided minority within the Fund vis-a-vis countries of great economic wealth. Thus, from its inception the Fund was biased against the poor countries. Paradoxically, the currencies of wealthy countries underwent the widest fluctuations but the severest damage from such fluctuations affected the underdeveloped and developing countries. (The purpose of the Fund, was, of course, to limit such fluctuations.)

In exchange for participation in the Fund any member state experiencing a temporary deficit in its balance of payments (that is, whenever the value of its imports exceeded the value of its exports) was entitled to buy, within certain limits the foreign currency it needed to restore balance while depositing a corresponding amount of local currency in the Fund. This privilege was called "drawing rights". Any country exercising such rights obligated itself to repurchase its deposits with the foreign currency previously acquired or with any of the other reserve currencies. As a result of this method of operation the International Monetary Fund became a "revolving fund" which bought and sold various currencies at fixed exchange rates but always preserved the total value of its monetary resources.

The forty-five countries that originally signed the agreement creating the Fund were subsequently joined by the remaining nations of the world, including the Soviet Union and other socialist bloc countries. However, the indisputable power of the United States at the time ensured that the world monetary system would be structured in accordance with the American plan to solve the problems of the war-ravaged industrial nations. There were two principal reasons why the participation of developing nations was minimal. The first was that the world still consisted of large colonial empires. The decolonization process and the rise of the new nations did not gather momentum until after World War II and stemmed from it in some respects. The second reason was the meager economic potential of some nations and the economic dependence of many nations which had recently become politically independent.

According to the prevailing American plan, the dollar was in effect the only currency that could be directly converted into gold at the fixed standard of $35 per ounce. The pound sterling, which was also a reserve fund, could only be converted through the dollar and its use was confined to the limits of the British Empire. Therefore, the ability of a country to meet the requirements of its international transactions depended on the gold or dollar reserves it held, either directly or through drawing rights on the International Monetary Fund. It subsequently became obvious, however, that the supply of gold and dollars was insufficient to give adequate liquidity to the system.

After the war no European country had the necessary resources for reconstruction and nearly all of them were indebted to the United States. As late as 1955, eight years after the Marshall Plan went into effect the indebtedness of the advanced capitalist countries to the U.S. reached 38 billion dollars—almost four and one-half times the total value of the monetary resources of the Fund. For this reason it has been appropriately said that the Marshall Plan—under which donations, credits, and transfers of capital to the European countries reached over 12 billion dollars—allowed the U.S. to lend chips to the other industrial nations so that they could continue gambling.

Under these circumstances, the United States deliberately initiated a deficit policy in its balance of payments in order to avoid the economic strangulation of other industrial nations, bearing in mind that the system could acquire liquidity only if they achieved a surplus in their balance of payments and accumulated dollars. As long as the U.S. maintained a substantial gold reserve exceeding the value of dollars in the possession of the foreign nations entitled at any time to request their conversion there was no problem; conversion was assured. But if the amount of dollars in the hands of foreign nations became so high as to endanger the possibility of conversion at the standard value of $35 per ounce of gold, the ensuing crisis of confidence would jeopardize the system's stability. Deficits in the U.S. balance of payments were moderate until 1958 but they became larger thereafter until in 1960 the dollar lost the stipulated parity and an ounce of gold was priced at $40. The revaluation of the German mark and of other European currencies in the 1960s worsened the dollar crisis to such a degree that the U.S. was forced to devaluate in 1971. On the European market the price per ounce of gold in December, 1974, was quoted at slightly over $195 which illustrates the depth of the dollar crisis and the degree to which the entire international monetary sysem was threatened.

The system's collapse became clearly evident in 1971 when the leading industrial nations modified the exchange rates of their currencies in complete disregard of the rules of the International Monetary Fund. Germany, fearing the effects of the world's inflationary process, revalued the mark by allowing it to "float". In that manner exports were discouraged, imports encouraged and the scarcity of commodities with its accompanying inflationary trend was alleviated.

However, the "coup de grace" to the system was left to President Nixon. He delivered it when he announced on August 15, 1971, that the convertibility of the dollar into gold was being suspended. Henceforth the U.S. would stop selling or buying gold, and the Bretton Woods system ceased to exist.

But if the system created at Bretton Woods proved vulnerable, it also became evident that it discriminated against many countries through the so-called "asymmetry of the decision-making apparatus". If a country had a deficit in its balance of payments over a long period of time it was forced to maintain a domestic deflationary policy and, in certain extreme cases of insufficient reserves it would reach the point of having to revaluate its currency. The only exception to this situation was the U.S., which had available any amount of dollars it needed since it was the origin of the system's basic currency. The asymmetry of the system was also evident in that countries with deficits could be forced to devaluate their currency; nothing, however, forced the countries with a surplus to revaluate theirs. In short, the international monetary system worked to the advantage of the strongest and to the disadvantage of the poorest nations.

It was upon this system that a great part of the world's economy depended until the 1960s, when the monetary crisis first became markedly apparent. The vulnerability of the system undoubtedly played an important role in intensification of the crisis, when four other factors came into play. First, the growing deficit in the U.S. balance of payments, accompanied by the dollar flight (which between 1959 and 1965 alone represented a drain of six billion dollars in gold), destroyed the capability to convert American currency into bullion at the fixed standard of $35 per ounce. Second, the growing economic power of the European countries and their free trade practices and capital transfers served to create a greater interdependence between their economies and currencies; a crisis in any one of them would, as a result, have severe repercussions in the others.

A third factor, closely linked to the two mentioned, was the appearance of the "Eurodollar" in the international capital market— a new foreign currency formed by several currencies, not necessarily by dollars or gold, but supported by convertibility into dollars. This new monetary unit contributed to greater fluidity in trade and currency exchange among the member states of the European Common Market by financing deficits and investments on a short-term basis. These techniques were distinctly beneficial to those countries but they also affected the devaluation of the dollar. Thus in 1948 the six countries of the Common Market had an available total of 2.68 billion in dollars and gold, while in 1957, ten years later, they had a reserve of 9.23 billion in dollars and gold.

Finally, the fourth factor was the realization among the developed European countries—especially the member states of the Common Market—that the system was unfavorable to them in comparison with the U.S. and that decision-making powers with respect to monetary matters were not commensurate with their newly acquired economic ascendancy. Partly because of this situation the so-called "Group of 10" was formed by the most developed non-communist nations: the United States, Japan, Great Britain, West Germany, France, Italy, Canada, the Netherlands, Belgium, and Sweden. As a body this group instantly superseded the International Monetary Fund; in effect it was in a position to make all the decisions.

After the Fund's system collapsed in 1971 a meeting was held at Washington's Smithsonian Institution for the purpose of finding a solution to the growing uncertainty and existing disorder in the currency exchange market. Monetary anarchy reigned despite the announcement by the International Monetary Fund that a temporary system of exchange rates would be instituted and despite statements by representatives of the Group of 10 calling for "a series of interrelated measures to reestablish the growth of international trade". Some countries, such as Mexico, decided to remain tied in parity to the dollar; others substantially devaluated their currencies in relation to the dollar; while others revaluated upward. Several non-Communist industrial countries chose to fix temporary central currency exchange rates.

The vicissitudes of the world's monetary system, the collapse of its stabilizing mechanisms in 1971, and the subsequent readjustment measures that were undertaken have served to demonstrate the need to democratize the International Monetary Fund. Although monetary problems and crises originate in the developed nations, the Fund's decisions should not respond exclusively to their interests, particularly since the Third World nations also bear the consequences. The reorganization of the international economic order will only be possible through a readjustment of the system to provide the developing nations with greater and more effective participation.

According to classic economic theory (considered in greatly simplified form), during what might be considered a period of normal economic activity the prices of some goods rise while others remain stable or decrease in response to the effects of supply and demand. During an inflationary period the prices of most goods and services rise simultaneously as demand for goods and services exceeds the quantity available. This demand occurs when the purchasing power rises—i.e., when both income and available cash increase. Thus, more money buys fewer goods and services, because as total income and available cash increase, each unit of currency is of less value.

The causes explaining the worldwide inflation that has pervaded the postwar economy cannot be dissociated from the two elements contributing to the crisis in the international order—the monetary system and the cold war.

Because of the cold war the military expenditures of both the United States and the Soviet Union, as well as other nations, were at a high level. These expenditures aided in maintaining low unemployment but by their very nature they are nonproductive expenditures. The cold war determined the existence of very high military appropriations which, without being productive, nevertheless distributed money that raised the general demand for goods services. This increased inflationary pressures, because although world demand for goods and services rose, the rate at which they were being supplied was considerably slower.

The problems of the international monetary system also seriously contributed to spiraling inflation: the relative scarcity of dollars in the international market, the loss of dollar convertibility, the prolonged deficit in the U.S. balance of payments, the appearance of Eurodollars, and the growing flow of capital and investments that augmented the amount of money in circulation. Other relevant factors included: the emergence of new nations with expectations for progress and a higher standard of living; foreign aid from "benefactor nations" to developing nations; the expansion of the so-called consumer society and of "consumerism" as a way of life; the energy crisis (which has become acute since the boycott by the Arab oil-producing nations); and the world-wide population explosion.

Following World War II practically all countries adopted policies providing or increasing aid to the poor, the unemployed, and the aged. This reordering of priorities demanded a productive system that existed in only a few nations. It was thought that the solution was economic growth and full employment and that prosperity would automatically spread throughout the population—a vain illusion that gave rise to policies of high social expenditures with an increase in world demand without a concurrent increase in productive capacity.

Even so, emergence of "benefactor nations" had the effect of lowering social, political and psychological tensions in some countries. Along with the reconstruction policies for industrial nations and the creation of international organizations that reinforced the dependence of underdeveloped countries on developed nations, such international aid was an important factor in attaining standards of living previously unknown and in creating systems of high-cost consumption. For most of the world, however, the presence of an unjust system of distribution of production and consumption has meant great effort rewarded by meager results. It is not an exaggeration to say that the prosperity of one part of the world has been built on the poverty of the other, although the latter is both territorially larger and more (heavily) populated.

The emergence of new nations and their legitimate expectations for improved standards of living, as well as the adoption of welfare concepts by the governments of "benefactor nations", increased the world demand for goods and services. Since many of the needed goods were not produced domestically by the new nations and their existing economic structures did not permit an expansion of production, the inevitable result was a gross increase in demand that has contributed to the general rise in prices.

Moreover, the desire for an "American way of life" not only has spread among the population of industrial nations, but has reached the wealthier social strata of the developing nations. Advertising and the so-called "demonstration effect" have increased demand for good and comfortable homes, for varied and abundant food, for fashionable clothes, for cars, stoves, refrigerators, television sets and electric appliances of all kinds, indoor plumbing, running water, electricity, adequate furniture, etc., along with the desire to acquire other less useful luxury goods. All these factors have led to the establishment of a culture of waste in a wide sector of the world population. The satisfaction of these needs (some basic and others superfluous), which modified the concept of poverty by making it socially intolerable and politically unacceptable, is one of the strongest inflationary pressures of our time.

As a consequence of the development of a consumer society there has been an unprecedented use of all kinds of natural resources, both renewable and nonrenewable. Some experts say that man has consumed more resources in this century than in all the thousands of years since his appearance on the face of the earth. Such indiscriminate consumption has led to a relative scarcity of some natural resources which have acquired great commercial value because of the great demand for them. As the price of these resources (one of which, oil, constitutes the driving force of industrial societies) goes up, the production costs of other goods have also risen. This situation, particularly with respect to nonrenewable natural resources which could have been foreseen ten or fifteen years ago (especially by consumer industrial nations that were not producers of these resources), became exceedingly critical when a group of oil-producing Arab nations decided to raise the price of their indispensable black gold˙and use it as a weapon in international political negotiations.

The world-wide repercussions of the energy crisis has most adversely affected the nations of the European Economic Community and Japan, for which the main source of oil is the Middle East. Simultaneously, the increasing economic interdependence of the world extended to other nations the effects of the inflationary measures adopted against some western nations by the Arab oil-producing countries. The inflationary process, however, has been more severe for non-oil-producing developing nations, which cannot absorb the rapid general increase in the cost of goods and services. Thus, the industrial nations hard hit by the oil crisis have transferred the greater part of their inflationary pressures to the dependent economies of developing nations.

The measures adopted by Arab nations and their union under the Organization of Petroleum Exporting Countries (OPEC) have accentuated the fact that the dependence between industrial nations and developing nations is mutual, although the advantages have in the past been exclusively on the side of the former. Industrial oil-consuming nations which at first reacted with the attitude of "every man for himself" — which caused widespread panic — have recently adopted an attitude of veiled threats and, under U. S. leadership, have declared that oil is the patrimony of the whole of mankind and not the exclusive property of a few nations. According to this concept, curiously enough, the resources of the developing nations needed by industrial countries are considered the universal patrimony of mankind but the production which these resources generate is solely the property of industrial nations and if the developing nations want them they must pay a very high price for them.

In the Third World there are internal factors—for example—the absence of integrated economic structures, backward technology, the lack of coordination between the productive and financial infrastructures, etc.—which help explain the phenomenon of persistent inflation. No analysis, however, would be complete if it ignored the inflationary impact on these countries of trade with the industrialized nations. The absence of an indigenous technology compels developing nations to turn to the developed nations, where the cost of technology includes the effects of inflation. Moreover, the industrial nations are in a position to transfer the cost of much of the world inflation to the underdeveloped nations in a variety of ways. While manufactured and consumer goods flowing from the industrial to the developing nations steadily continue to cost more, the price of raw materials rises less rapidly or even drops, in the international market. This is a result of the defective structure and operation of the international market, the economic dependence of the nations of the Third World, and the practices of great multinational or supranational organizations that operate with increasing ease in the industrial economy of the advanced nations. In short, this means, that the trading advantage is held predominantly by the economically powerful nations.

The new polarization in the world economic system between industrial and developing nations — which, incidentally, the Economic Commission for Latin America (ECLA) refers to as "central" and "peripheral" respectively—is particularly evident in the pattern of commercial relations during the most recent quarter of this century. While the average level of exports from developed nations increased by 8.6% per annum, that of the developing nations rose by 5.3%, the lowest percentage being that of Latin America, which rose by only 3.8%. This means that the role of the Third World in international trade decreased both consistently and considerably: from 30% in 1948 to 21% in 1960, and 17% during 1970. Two basic reasons explain this decline; first, the constant deterioration in the terms of trade between developing countries and developed nations; second, the relative decline in the commercial transactions of the Third World, chiefly because the developed nations trade more with each other (between 1948 and 1970, trade between developed nations rose from 64% to 77% of the world total). The immediate consequence of this situation was to reinforce the uniform international division of labor between nations producing industrial goods and nations producing raw materials and food. In its turn, this involves a greater interdependence between the two and not a greater independence for developed nations, as might be assumed. The energy crisis and the Arab boycott clearly heightened the growing interdependence between the industrial and the developing world. Awareness of this interdependence has aroused new expectations and hopes for progress among the nations of the Third World which look upon the sovereign use of their resources as a way to obtain, on the basis of real equality and in a fair exchange with industrial nations, the technology and financial resources they need for development.

Another factor that helps explain the phenomenon of worldwide inflation is the marked increase of demand for all manner of economic goods for a population that is growing at an incredible rate.

3: Fallout Factors
of the Population Explosion

Some experts say that our ancestors first appeared on this planet more than four million years ago. We do not know the precise time but we do know that hundreds of thousands of years passed before the human population reached the level of 500 million in the 18th century. Subsequently the earth's population began to grow steadily but with increasing momentum; by the middle of the last century it was over a billion; less than a hundred years later, around 1930, there were approximately two billion people inhabiting the earth.

Although a great many years went by before the world's population reached the billion mark, it took less than a century for that figure to double. By 1930 humanity was multiplying at a dizzying speed; forty-five years later it had doubled. Today the world's population is close to four billion. Another doubling is expected to occur within thirty years or so. In short, the rate of population growth has taken on an explosive nature. The present growth rate is 2% per annum; by the year 2000 the earth will probably be inhabited by more than seven billion human beings.

The extraordinary growth of world population is primarily the result of advances in science and technology which have enabled man to triumph over disease and early death, thus doubling or tripling the average number of years a person may live. The population explosion is unquestionably the most tangible evidence of the triumph of our species over nature.

While both child and adult mortality have decreased and life expectancy has increased, fertility has tended to remain the same or to decline more slowly than the death rate: hence the rapid growth characteristic of the present-day world population. However, there is a marked difference between the fertility rates of developed and developing countries. While the fertility rate of developed nations has passed through a period demographers call transitional and has diminished to the level of the death rate — thus establishing a population with a growth rate of about 1% per annum — the nations of the Third World, just entering the phase of reduced mortality, are experiencing a high fertility rate. This explains the disproportionate population growth of the Third World — 2.8% per annum or three times that of developed nations.

There is a close relationship between fecundity and the various aspects of national development—education, culture and information, economic resources for the purchase of contraceptives, a more secular attitude toward sex, equality of opportunity for men and women, etc.

National development does not, of course, automatically cause a decline in the birth rate; demographic phenomena, being cumulative, do not tend to produce results until 15 or 20 years after they have been acted upon, even directly, but the general effect of development has been a reduction in the birth rate and, consequently, relative stability in population growth.

Even though an accelerated rate of population growth does not in itself constitute a problem, it becomes serious in the light of the resources and productive capacity required to provide essential economic goods. It is a fact that more than two people are born per second, which means 80 million new mouths to feed and bodies to clothe each year. These human beings need not only food and clothing, but also employment, education, hospitals, recreation, and other goods and services.

Understandably, the standard of living is not the same in all parts of the world. The population is not distributed equally over its surface and the growth rate is not similar in all areas and countries. But before analyzing the structure, dynamics, and diffusion of the world's population, we must take into account the significance of the present-day population level and its implications for the economic, political and social order.

The life of an inhabitant of the industrial world is vastly different from that of an inhabitant of a developing agrarian society. Yet there is a bond between them: both are human beings and both have some hope of improving their standard of living. They may differ as to what they consider optimum living conditions and even the methods of attaining them but both would like to live better. In great measure their hopes are determined by their immediate experiences in the world they know. The advent of technological changes has wiped out old natural boundaries; the mass communications media, for example, have made the poverty of some appear much less bearable in comparison with the opulence of others. For some people a fundamental problem is how to eat a great deal without gaining weight; for an inhabitant of the Third World the problem is to find enough food so as not to die of hunger. National life styles and patterns of consumption did not differ greatly in the 18th century; in recent times the industrial revolution has created a gap separating poor nations from rich nations—a gap which keeps widening daily.

While the population of the industrial countries is less than a third of the world total, two-thirds of the earth's people live in developing or underdeveloped nations. Moreover, the population of the Third World is increasing at a rate three times greater than that of the industrial countries. In a very short time, by the beginning of the next century, nearly four-fifths of humanity will populate nations which we now consider developing or underdeveloped. From this perspective, the much worn out terms of the cold war regarding "capitalism" and "communism" have obviously lost their meaning.

The present division of the world is that of a rich minority living in industrial countries versus the Third World's growing mass of humanity in various stages of indigence and hunger. One must not lose sight of the fact that even though strides by Third

World countries resulted in an economic growth rate between 1950 and 1970 which was slightly higher (5% per annum) than that of the developed nations (4.7% per annum) — despite the obstacles due to the international economic system — these strides are frustrated by a population explosion of enormous proportions. In considering the economic growth rate from a demographic point of view, the productivity rate of increase per inhabitant between 1950 and 1970 was 2.5% in Third World countries versus 3.5% for the industrial world. Under such conditions the Third World's population growth inevitably disrupts its development and widens the gap separating it from the industrial world.

Significantly, almost half the inhabitants of the Third World are under 15 years of age. In a few years their number will be greater than that of the entire population of the industrial world. Since children and adolescents are necessarily economically unproductive, they are dependent on the so-called active economic population, technically known as population density, does not contunities for the development of the Third World. Billions of young people exert an enormous pressure on education and jobs; but they also constitute a source of strength if the growth of Third World nations is speeded up.

Elimination of the abuses of the present international order is clearly essential in order to permit an equitable distribution of the benefits of development. No great effort of imagination is needed to visualize the alternative: tremendous pressure of billions of people on a steadily weakening international structure.

Population by itself, of course, cannot be equated with national prosperity. Much necessarily depends upon the use of natural resources and production for the purpose of raising material and cultural living standards. Likewise, the ratio of land area to population, techincally known as population density, does not constitute an indicator of a nation's standard of living; urbanization has subverted this concept. Indeed, a greater or lesser population density has no meaning when seen from the viewpoint of urbanization. A large urban concentration can guarantee extraordinary levels of material and cultural comfort or, conversely, provide the impetus for constant deterioration in living conditions. The reason for this is that population — its growth and distribution— is only meaningful within its social, economic, political and cultural context.

It should also be noted that urban concentration has progressed at a faster pace than population growth and its consequences are not the same for all areas and countries. In 1950 approximately 700 million of the world's population—27.5%—lived in cities. Today more than one billion and 300 million persons inhabit cities. By the year 2000 half the population of this planet will be urban. Even in this regard, however, valid conclusions cannot be made without first pointing out the differences between the Third World and the industrial nations. In 1950 half the populations of the latter lived in cities; today they number two-thirds of the population; by the year 2000 they will constitute four-fifths of the inhabitants of industrial nations. In general this population has the benefit of all, or at least most, of the urban services.

The situation of Third World nations is quite different. In 1950 only 15.5% of its population was urban and at present only one-fourth is urban. By the year 2000 more than 40% of its population will live in cities. But population concentrations in Third World cities are more serious because overcrowding is accompanied by shanty towns and shacks where the deterioration of material and moral conditions is steadily growing. In some Third World countries, where most of the population is widely scattered, the provision of services and the use of technology to increase production is minimal. This problem is aggravated by a persistent exodus to cities unable to absorb the labor flowing into them and incapable of providing the services that high urban concentration requires. It is very significant, for example, that between one-fifth and one-fourth of the population of Third World countries is clustered in their capital cities. While there were 24 cities with more than a million inhabitants in developing countries in 1950, there are more than 80 such cities today. By 1985 the Third World will have more than 150 cities with populations of over a million and their total inhabitants will exceed 470 million persons.

This population displacement not only takes place from the rural to the urban areas within one country but also occurs between nations. Moreover, displacement causes serious problems for underdeveloped countries because the migrating population is generally composed of economically active and, in many cases, more skilled workers. Another example of the dependence of poor nations on rich nations is that technical knowledge does not become widespread but is concentrated in a few large, generally multinational companies.

In analyzing the demographic pattern of today's world the increasing importance of food production cannot be ignored. Although some of the following pages will be dedicated to the food crisis that our troubled world is now enduring, at the moment we will merely point out the enormous discrepancy between available arable land and the percentage of the population dependent on agriculture in both industrial and Third World nations. Without going into the differences in technology, which obviously increase the gap between them, the present-day situation can be summed up as follows: while in 1970 more than 65% of the Third World population was engaged in agriculture on arable land totalling 7.3 million square kilometers, only 19% of the population of industrial nations was engaged in agriculture and had seven million square kilometers of arable land at its disposal. This means that while in the Third World there are 226 people per square kilometer trying to wrest a living from the land with the help of a backward technology and rudimentary knowledge, in the developed nations there are 51 persons working each square kilometer of arable land assisted by high levels of technology. The direct consequence of this situation is apparent in the great discrepancies between their respective productivity. The agricultural producer in the industrial world produces more per hectare, more per person, more per everything.

This is the demographic situation we now face at the international level. There is no doubt that the number of persons, their distribution, age structure and the population growth rate has had important consequences for the establishment of a new international order and has exerted a great influence in hastening the collapse of the order established at Yalta after the second World War. Population by itself is certainly incapable of producing specific consequences, but combined with the other political and economic factors we have been discussing, it has helped to precipitate the crisis. The population explosion cannot be held responsible for the deterioration of the environment.

The pollution of the atmosphere and the seas has primarily been the product of rapid industrial development. While the developed nations remain chiefly responsible for the pollution of the environment, the consequences are felt to a large degree by all inhabitants of the earth. It would, of course, be absurd to think that a return to the artisan form of production is in order, or that industrial development should be arrested. The nations of the Third World cannot be expected to forego industrialization and accept the conditions of poverty in which their populations live at the same time that industrial nations continue to enjoy their present high standard of living.

It is true that in the last few years rising concern over the pollution of the environment has persuaded some industrial nations to devote some of their enormous resources to pollution control. But antipollutant technology is so expensive that developing nations cannot absorb its cost. For these countries industrial progress and environmental pollution constitute a dilemma since these nations cannot pass up industrial progress nor avail themselves of the sophisticated antipollution technology of the developed nations. Moreover, it is disquieting to note that branch companies of multinational corporations situated in Third World nations act irresponsibly by resorting to wasteful technological practices—i.e., practices which because of their polluting nature have been severely restricted in the industrial country of origin. Internal combustion engines prohibited or allowed only with modifications in industrial countries continue, for example, to be actively sold in developing nations.

Judging by the lofty declarations of developed nations their concern over pollutants could well be termed "lese-humanité." But it is important to note that none of the existing international organizations is making any effort to require industrial countries which transfer technologies to the Third World nations to act responsibly.

The great disparity in consumption that exists between the rich and poor populations of the world suggests an enormous discrepancy also in the relative quantity of pollutants they contribute to the environment. It is estimated that an inhabitant of the industrial world pollutes 14 times more than his counterpart in the Third World, since both the energy used and wasted to maintain a high level of consumption are greater in industrial countries. Thus the consumerism of industrial nations is the real cause of ecological deterioration—not, as some contend, the Third World's population explosion. The rapid population growth of developing countries exerts a direct influence in other respects, as we have already shown, and relates to this subject only indirectly.

Parallel to growing concern over environmental degeneration is an awareness that many of the resources of the earth are finite. Experts in such matters calculate that man has consumed two or three times more resources in the last century than in the hundreds of thousands of years since his evolution on this planet. Obviously, consumption has been and continues to be proportionately greater in industrial nations. But as many of these resources—in the form of foodstuffs or raw materials for industry—come from underdeveloped nations the international order imposed by the developed nations presupposes the existence of an

international division of labor in which some countries produce
raw materials and food while others produce industrial goods.
This division of labor, firmly established among the countries of
the Warsaw Pact as well as so-called Western nations, has often
been denounced by nations struggling to attain industrial progress and is another reason why the present international balance
is so precarious. This does not constitute a prelude to a third
World War but demonstrates that the world order as a whole
is facing a serious crisis on many fronts. It is imperative to
take this crisis into account and to establish a new order in
which the prosperity of some countries is not based on the misery
of the rest. Developed nations should heed what John F. Kennedy
said when he became President of the United States: "If a free
society cannot help the many who are poor, it will not be able to
save the few who are rich."

N.B

The unjust international division of labor has contributed in
a significant way to the ecological imbalance of our planet. This
division has tended to burden Third World nations with monoculture economics in which essentially only a single plant species
(e.g., bananas) is grown commercially. Monoculture quickly impairs the quality of the land, eroding it and contributing to
the deterioration of the ecosystem.

More importantly, the third of the world population which
lives in the industrial nations consumes two-thirds of the earth's
food, and the rest of the world barely obtains one-third of this
food. Thus developing nations suffer a chronic quantitative and
qualitative hunger. While the inhabitant of a rich country consumes a daily average of 3,000 calories and 95 grams of protein
(of which 30 grams are animal protein), his counterpart in the
Third World barely consumes, on the average, 2,300 calories and
60 grams of protein (six grams of which are animal protein).
In the so-called "hunger zones" these figures are, of course, much
lower. Of the two billion 700 million human beings that present-
ly live in the developing nations, 700 million do not have sufficient
food, and more than one and a half billion do not get qualitatively

adequate food. Undernourished, they fall prey to all manner of diseases. It is estimated that at least twelve million people, most of them children, annually die in the Third World as a direct consequence of hunger or malnutrition. Given the present population level, it is asserted that if after 1975 there are two successive bad harvests in Asia or Latin America more than 200 million people are likely to die of hunger.

Underdevelopment and economic dependence are principal elements in this international tragedy. The following factors contribute to their existence in Third World nations: lack of knowledge and adequate technology, shortage of fertilizers and irrigation, the relatively low quality of land under cultivation, the lack of organization in production, and nonexistent or limited agricultural infrastructure.

In recent years a process has taken place which cannot be ignored. Immediately after World War II Latin America was the area with the world's greatest grain surplus; at present it is obliged to import grain. Ten years ago the total world grain reserves (including those of developed nations) were 225 million metric tons; at present they are down to 80 million tons. In view of the world's increasing consumption of grain, uneven as it is, there are today only enough reserves for a bare three months.

The food crisis highlights the need for a World Food and Agricultural Research Bank of the type Dr. Echeverria proposed to the Food and Agriculture Organization of the United Nations in an address he delivered in 1974.

The need for a new law of the sea is intimately linked to the food crisis and the preservation of both the environment and our resources. At the United Nations Conference on the Law of the Sea held in Caracas in July, 1974, Mexico recommended recognition of "territorial seas" extending 12 miles from the shores of coastal nations and expansion of economic jurisdictions to a distance of 200 miles. Thus a coastal nation could not exercise full sovereignty in the zone between 12 and 200 miles from its shores but would have control over the resources within this zone. Unfortunately this proposal has been the cause of friction between the developing countries, some of which have extensive maritime areas, and developed countries which prefer unrestricted exploitation of sea resources everywhere.

Awareness of these related problems in industrial nations has given rise to a number of reports which vary in their interpretations of the postwar international crises and in their proposed solutions.

The Club of Rome—a group of international scientists, businessmen, and politicians—is the sponsor of a report originally entitled *The Predicament of Mankind* and prepared by a group of scholarly experts who drew heavily on the computer facilities of the Massachusetts Institute of Technology. Significantly, when their book was published in the United States several years ago it appeared under the revealing title *The Limits of Growth.*

The Club of Rome's study, an attempt to provide a technocratic explanation of current problems, sidesteps the political and moral aspects of these problems. Its central thesis, stripped of circumlocution, is roughly as follows: As a result of the population explosion and its effects on per capita consumption, there is an enormous pressure on the earth's limited resources, particularly the generation or regeneration capacity of the ecological system so indispensable for human existence. This pressure, it is contended, won't let up until the general equilibrium of man and his environment is restored through a catastrophic decrease in the world's population within approximately 60 years—unless, perchance, present trends undergo drastic alteration. Said catastrophe, the report warns, will manifest itself in massive mortality and an irreversible deterioration of man's material and cultural life.

N.b   The five problems analyzed in the Club of Rome report are: (1) population growth, (2) the production of food, (3) environmental pollution, (4) industrial growth, and (5) depletion of non-renewable natural resources. By manipulating the facts about these problems with carefully chosen hypotheses the authors come to the unequivocal conclusion that there is no possibility that existing resources will be able to sustain the 14 billion people expected to populate our planet in the coming century. Ergo, the only alternative is to encourage drastic reduction of population growth.

The Club of Rome report also says that it is impossible for the majority of the inhabitants of developing nations to achieve the standard of living now enjoyed by the citizens of developed nations. Indeed, the report predicts that living standards in the industrial world are likely to decline rapidly during the next four or five decades. Therefore, given the fact that the natural equilibrium of the ecological system has been upset, man will have to severely limit his economic and population growth or face dire consequences.

Apart from the report's questionable scientific validity and the methodology used by its authors, it has many weaknesses. It makes no effort for example, to deal with viable methods by which to avoid the dreadful catastrophe it envisions. Moreover, by ignoring the complex political and moral implications, the authors fall into what may be aptly described as a rationalization of the international status quo in the light of the existing world order.

A distinctly optimistic counterpart of the Club of Rome study is the report issued by the Commission for the year 2000, a body created under the patronage of two major American corporations. By marshalling a fascinating melange of facts, the authors of this study discover the existence of what they call a "multiple [world] tendency" which has convinced them that although the world in general will continue to progress, the underdeveloped nations will be unable to achieve the present level of well being enjoyed by the peoples of industrial nations because the gap separating them will continue to widen as a result of the accelerated population growth which operates as a hindrance to the progress of the poor nations. While conceding that international bipolarity will sharpen simultaneously with the proliferation of nuclear weapons, the authors of the report reject the possibility of a third World War simply on the ground that they are confident the dominant powers will prefer to co-exist peacefully for the indefinite future.

Unlike the authors of the Club of Rome, the writers of the report prepared for the Commission for the Year 2000 have a somewhat broader point of view in that they at least take into account some political and sociological considerations. But with regard to the differences between rich and poor nations, the Commission's authors, like the Club's writers, accept the tacit premise that the present international order will remain intact and doesn't have to change much. Statistically the Commission's report would be unobjectionable if the facts on which the authors base their premise were complete or accurate. Their optimistic conclusion is that multiple tendencies will in the long run lead to the development of desirable materialistic cultures, the establishment of middle-class and democratic elites, the spread of technological and scientific knowledge, worldwide distribution of industrial capabilities, increasing opulence and leisure, the growth of large urban concentrations, higher literacy and education, and a decline in the importance of primary and secondary economic production in favor of "tertiary" and "quaternary" forms. This Pollyanna conclusion utterly ignores the potentialities and consequences of inflation, unemployment, the lag of food production behind population growth, and the limited usefulness of international organizations as ameliorative instruments.

The Commission's optimistic study, focused primarily on the positive aspects of growth, preceded the Apocalyptic vision evoked by the Club of Rome report. Perhaps the explanation for the different outlooks of the reports is that they were written five years apart. In any case, one cannot help but notice that the attitude of both reports toward underdeveloped nations is essentially similar. In analyzing world conditions both virtually ignored not only the needs and expectations of these nations but also the disparity in development levels between rich and poor countries and the fact that the problems faced by Third World nations are not equivalent to the experience of industrial powers. While the authors of both reports recognize that all nations inhabit the same planet and concede that developed nations have responsibilities to other countries with which they share the planet, they forget that the developing nations must break out of their restrictive shells.

Less pretentious, but much more perceptive, is the work of Claus Jacoby, *The Human Deluge*. Following a brief analysis of population characteristics, he points out the effects of food scarcity, rising discontent, and related factors. He goes on to discuss the problems developed nations face with respect to the human flood inundating the Third World and the ominous consequences this entails for the prosperity of rich nations and the world order in general. He concludes that there are two alternatives: either poor nations should be confined and quarantined or a suitable method of international cooperation must be found.

If the first alternative is chosen, the rich nations, convinced that it is impossible to save the entire world from catastrophe, would presumably feel they should save themselves by building a powerful economic, political and military retaining wall to prevent invasion from hungry peoples. The rich nations would then be able to relax tensions among themselves, particularly the vestiges of cold war tensions and dedicate their energies to the protection of their prosperity instead of wasting it in pointless acts of charity toward the poor nations. Although this option is morally unacceptable, even to rich nations, it is, of course, politically and militarily impractical. Economically, however, it might be viable. Rich nations have agricultural surpluses, great oil reserves, and other nonrenewable resources. By strengthening the economies of countries with great development potential, from whom they would be able to obtain needed raw materials, they would indeed be in a position to build a retaining wall against the hungry masses of the world.

Rich countries enjoy an unquestioned military superiority but they no longer have the protection of nuclear monopoly. China, India, and other nations today have impressive nuclear capability for reprisals. The use of atomic weapons in any part of the world is bound to cause irreparable damage, directly and indirectly, to all nations, rich and poor alike, if only because of the inevitability of ecological fallout. Politically, the quarantine solution is not feasible because the frontiers of the world are much smaller today and mass communications can penetrate all areas.

The poverty, hunger, ignorance, and irrepressible discontent of two-thirds of mankind cannot, of course, be neglected. The rich nations must realize that the only realistic alternative is international cooperation based on justice and nondependence. Only by acting simultaneously on all fronts to hasten the development of the Third World nations will it be possible to double food production, raise education levels, provide more employment and build more hospitals and homes, etc., within the 35 year period in which the population is expected to double.

The four critical areas, as Dr. Jacoby points out, are education, industrial development, food production, and birth control. There is no room for failure in any of them but much depends on decisions and actions taken at national levels as well as on the judicial and administrative instruments through which effective international cooperation can be achieved.

Perhaps the most stark presentation of the confinement option appears in "Famine—1975", a book by William and Paul Paddock published in 1967 under the subtitle "America's Decision: Who Will Survive?" This book provides a detailed analysis of the most crucial problems: population and hunger. The authors place the Third World nations into three categories: nations which will survive without help, nations which will not survive despite all possible help, and nations which will only survive if they are helped. On the basis of their criteria, the Paddock brothers conclude that international cooperation and bilateral help from the rich nations should be exclusively given to the last category. They are apathetic toward the nations imperiled by their classification.

Even without considering the social and moral consequences of the Paddock brothers' solution, its applicability is doomed to failure by reason of its military, political, and economic implications.

A fifth book that cannot be disregarded is Irving S. Freedman's *Inflation: Worldwide Disaster*. It analyzes the social, economic, and political causes of inflation, concludes that it is a phenomenon of the international economic configuration, and discusses various means by which to surmount it. The author is unable to resist the temptation to present his views with respect to what he considers the need for developing nations to establish an "acceptable level of poverty". He contends that by maintaining their expectations for satisfaction of higher consumer levels the developing nations increase world demand without making substantial contributions in the area of production. He also urges reduction of consumption by the people of industrial nations in order to combat world inflationary tendencies. This proposal cannot be equated with his suggestion that three-fourths of the earth's inhabitants are doomed to live at an "acceptable level of poverty". While the high consumption of industrial nations can be lowered without affecting their standard of living, there is no leeway in regard to the subsistence consumption levels of the Third World, especially in the most underdeveloped nations.

A more general book concerned with the political aspects of the international order—which cannot be dissociated from the economic substratum—is a French work by Alexandre Faire and Jean-Paul Sebord entitled *Le Nouveau Desequilibre Mondial* (The New World Imbalance), published shortly before the oil crisis disrupted the European economy. After analyzing four factors— relations between the United States and Europe, European unity, the economic rise of Japan, and the oil resources of the Arab nations—the authors conclude that we are living in a period of great imbalance which will tend to intensify in the absence of short-term prospects for reconciling the four factors on which the balance of the world rests. Some of the Third World nations are considered factors in this balance solely by virtue of their oil.

From the ethnocentric European perspective, as this book shows, the developing nations remain essentially colonized and dependent entities. This is not surprising since European industrial nations continue to think solely in terms of their own problems without regard to those of the Third World. For them "the world is Europe" rather than "Europe is part of the world".

4: Challenges for
Developing Nations

Since its creation in the early 1960s the United Nations Conference on Trade and Development has been the principal international forum where developing and developed nations present their points of view and explore methods for regulating trade between producers of raw materials and producers of industrial goods.

The years which have elapsed since the first UNCTAD meeting took place have revealed enormous differences between the interests of industrial nations and those of the Third World. On the whole, the meetings of the conference have provided an eminently useful forum for the discussion of problems that have too long been sidestepped—especially those involving the economic and technological dependence of developing nations on industrial countries, and the obstacles to independent development arising out of dependence.

It was at the third conference in 1972 that Dr. Echeverria made his historic proposal for the formulation of principles and rules of international law for the world's economic relations. In 1974 this proposal, metamorphosed into the Charter of Economic Rights and Duties of States, was adopted by the United Nations General Assembly. The charter is intimately linked with the United Nations Conference on Trade and Development not only because it was proposed at that forum but also because it embodies many of the aspirations Third World nations have voiced at its sessions.

From its inception the conference has generally been split into three blocs of nations that have tended to reflect less cohesion at each meeting: developed industrial nations with a market economy (U.S.-NATO bloc), nations with planned economies (Soviet bloc), and developing nations. Too often there has been confrontation between the industrial capitalist nations and the developing nations while socialist countries have looked on from the sidelines.

The late 1950s and early 1960s were years of profound disillusionment for Third World nations, many of which gained their independence amid high hopes that have since been frustrated. A key reason for frustration was the low prices they received for the raw materials that were the main source of their income. In addition, although international financial assistance increased substantially, interest charges on early credits and loans remained so high that the beneficial effects of aid were practically cancelled out. In consequence, top priority economic and social improvements became unattainable.

Other problems included the dependency of underdeveloped nations on the developed ones for urgently needed products and the use of disadvantageous "credit packages" under which a nation selling raw materials became obligated to buy manufactured goods from the purchaser rather than from the general world market. Indeed, the very structure of international economic arrangements and the international economic system tended to hinder independent development.

The idea gradually spread among the underdeveloped nations that basic changes in the international trade system were imperative. One aspect of this was the feeling that developing as well as developed nations should jointly help shape international financial policy, particularly because of the inefficiency of the United Nations' economic agencies and the lack of coordination among the various international trade organizations and the international monetary institutions created at Bretton Woods.

Thus from pessimism, frustration, and resentment an atmosphere of confrontation evolved at United Nations forums during the 1960's although many factors favored unity among developing nations. Often they were impeded by the blocs representing both the planned economies and the industrial nations. Inevitably, disunity among the developing nations fostered their manipulation.

On December 19, 1961, the United Nations General Assembly approved Resolution 1710 entitled the "United Nations Development Decade" and Resolution 1707 named "International Trade as an Instrument for Economic Development." The latter called attention to the urgent need to raise the value of the exports of developing nations and called upon the Secretary General of the UN to consult member nations about the desirability of holding an international conference on world trade concerned especially with basic commodities. Subsequently, on August 3, 1962, the UN Economic and Social Council, agreed to convene a Conference on Trade and Development, and it established a commission of experts to prepare an agenda and the necessary documentation. In endorsing the Council's decision (December, 1962), the UN General Assembly set forth the basic points to be considered at the projected conference:

"(a) The need for increasing the trade of developing countries in primary commodities as well as in semi-manufactured and manufactured goods so as to ensure a rapid expansion of their export earnings and, for that purpose, to examine the possibility of taking measures and reformulating principles with a view to: increasing trade between the developing and developed countries, irrespective of the differences in the foreign trade systems of the latter; intensifying trade relations among the developing countries; diversifying the trade of developing countries; financing the international trade of developing countries;

"(b) Measures for ensuring stable, equitable and remunerative prices and the rising demand for exports of developing countries, including, *inter alia*; the stabilization of prices of primary commodities at equitable and remunerative levels; the increase in consumption of products imported from primary-materials producing countries and of semi-manufactured and manufactured goods imported from developing countries; international commodity agreements; international compensatory financing;

"(c) Measures leading to the gradual removal of tariff, non-tariff or other trade barriers by industrialized countries, whether individually or collectively, which have an adverse effect on the exports of developing countries and on the expansion of international trade in general;

"(d) Methods and machinery to implement measures relating to the expansion of international trade, including; a reappraisal of the effectiveness of the existing international bodies dealing with international trade in meeting trade problems of developing countries, including a consideration of the development of trade relations among countries with uneven levels of economic development and/or different systems of economic organization and trade; the advisability of eliminating overlapping and duplication by co-ordination or consolidation of the activities of such bodies, of creating conditions for expanded membership, and of effecting such other organizational improvements and initiatives as may be needed, so as to maximize the beneficial results of trade for the promotion of economic development."

Although these objectives were quite broad, the fact that the UN General Assembly adopted them by unanimous consent gave rise to the feeling that the conferences would produce useful results. In any case, for the first time in history there was to be an international forum at which the differences between rich and poor nations could be publicly discussed.

In keeping with the Assembly's recommendations, the UN Economic and Social Council broadened membership of the preparatory commission to include 32 nations. The commission held three sessions in 1963 and 1964, two in New York and one in Geneva. During this period, at the Council's request the UN's various economic commissions and other international organizations cooperated in preparing the documents to be discussed at the first UNCTAD conference.

In one of the basic documents, "Towards a New Trade Policy in Favor of Development", Dr. Raul Prebisch, Secretary General of the conference, warned that "it is imperative to begin building a new world economic order to help solve the serious trade and development problems of the world in general, and especially those which afflict developing nations . . . the conference must address itself particularly to . . . the persistent tendency towards trade imbalance arising during economic development. While, generally speaking, the demand for primary commodity goods—with very few exceptions—grows relatively slowly, the demand for manufactured goods rises directly with development. The resulting imbalance is a great factor in the strangulation of development. It is essential to correct this imbalance to enable development to proceed under dynamic and stable conditions."

With regard to the "United Nations Development Decade" resolution seeking a minimum annual growth rate of 5 percent in the income of developing nations by 1970, Dr. Prebisch pointed out that in spite of the relatively modest rate desired this would be exceedingly difficult to attain "for a great number of developing nations . . . if this conference does not give rise to a policy of international cooperation, primarily designed to eliminate the trade imbalance . . ."

What has not been sufficiently understood is that underdevelopment is the result of economic dependence. Traditionally development was thought of as a sequential economic process rather than one entailing social and organizational change. Although it was clear that the gap between rich and poor countries was widening during the 1960's, some experts thought this was the result of the vast technological revolution which had taken place in the rich nations. It was not realized that the industrial revolution had transformed the *entire* world, encouraging socioeconomic systems in industrial nations capable of generating a self-supporting dynamic growth while at the same time creating dependent systems in the remaining nations.

*   *   *

The confrontation between rich and poor countries came to a head at the first United Nations Conference on Trade and Develop-

ment held in Geneva in 1964. In addressing the conference, UN
Secretary General U Thant highlighted the need for its sessions:

"The post-war period witnessed the fundamental reorientation
of the people of the underdeveloped world. Today, there is hardly
an underdeveloped area on earth where the people are not aware
of the existence of the opulent societies . . . Thus the conditions
prevailing in their own countries are no longer acceptable . . . This
growth of a new social consciousness has necessitated a new approach to the international economy; it has created a dramatic
need for rapid economic development of the less-developed areas,
for the improvement of agriculture, and for the acceleration of the
process of industralization. It has also become obvious that a new
international division of labor is required. Furthermore, the emergence of the socialist countries [as industrial nations] creates
strong reasons for their fuller integration into the international
economy. . . .

"The contrast between the developed and the underdeveloped
parts of the world . . . awareness of this contrast [with a] political
awakening [and] continued economic bondage and poverty . . . are
the premises which in my view constitute the real background of
this conference."

In concluding his speech Dr. U Thant expressed a fervent wish
that was not fulfilled until the United Nations approved the Charter
of Economic Rights and Duties of States in 1974. His prophetic
words remain relevant today: "The least you should do is to provide humanity, both in the underdeveloped and developed countries, with a set of principles and policies to make trade a genuine
instrument of progress toward economic development, thus helping to secure universal prosperity and peace for this and succeed-
ing generations."

The conference endorsed 15 general and 13 special principles
regarding international trade and development policies. Although
these principles were somewhat general in nature and did not
immediately acquire the status of a United Nations resolution,
they became the basis for Dr. Echeverria's proposal for the

Charter of Economic Rights and Duties of States approved by the General Assembly ten years later. The general principles recommended by the conference were as follows:

1. "Economic relations between countries, including trade relations, shall be based on respect for the principle of sovereign equality of States, self-determination of peoples, and non-interference in the internal affairs of other countries.

2. "There shall be no discrimination on the basis of the differences in socio-economic systems. Adaptation of trading methods shall be consistent with this principle.

3. "Every country has the sovereign right freely to trade with other countries, and freely to dispose of its natural resources in the interest of the economic development and well-being of its own people.

4. "Economic development and social progress should be the common concern of the whole international community and should, by increasing economic prosperity and well-being, help strengthen peaceful relations and co-operation among nations. Accordingly, all countries pledge themselves to pursue internal and external economic policies designed to accelerate economic growth throughout the world, and in particular to help promote, in developing countries, a rate of growth consistent with the need to bring about a substantial and steady increase in average income, in order to narrow the gap between the standard of living in developing countries and that in the developed countries.

5. "National and international economic policies should be directed towards the attainment of an international division of labour in harmony with the needs and interests of developing countries in particular, and of the world as a whole. Developed countries should assist the developing countries in their efforts to speed up their economic and social progress, should co-operate in measures taken by developing countries for diversifying their economies, and should encourage appropriate adjustments in their own economies to this end.

6. "International trade is one of the most important factors in

economic development. It should be governed by such rules as are consistent with the attainment of economic and social progress and should not be hampered by measures incompatible therewith. All countries should co-operate in creating conditions of international trade conducive, in particular, to the achievement of a rapid increase in the export earnings of developing countries and, in general, to the promotion of an expansion and diversification of trade between all countries, whether at similar levels of development, at different levels of development, or having different economic and social systems.

7. "The expansion and diversification of international trade depends upon increasing access to markets, and upon remunerative prices for the exports of primary products. Developed countries shall progressively reduce and eliminate barriers and other restrictions that hinder trade and consumption of products from developing countries and take positive measures such as will create and increase markets for the exports of developing countries. All countries should co-operate through suitable international arrangements, on an orderly basis, in implementing measures designed to increase and stabilize primary commodity export earnings, particularly of developing countries, at equitable and remunerative prices and to maintain a mutually acceptable relationship between the prices of manufactured goods and those of primary products.

8. "International trade should be conducted to mutual advantage on the basis of the most-favoured-nation treatment and should be free from measures detrimental to the trading interests of other countries. However, developed countries should grant concessions to all developing countries and extend to developing countries all concessions they grant to one another and should not, in granting these or other concessions, require any concessions in return from developing countries. New preferential concessions, both tariff and non-tariff, should be made to developing countries as a whole and such preferences should not be extended to developed countries. Developing countries need not extend to developed countries preferential treatment in operation amongst them. Special preferences

at present enjoyed by certain developing countries in certain developed countries should be regarded as transitional and subject to progressive reduction. They should be eliminated as and when effective international measures guaranteeing at least equivalent advantages to the countries concerned come into operation.

9. "Developed countries participating in regional economic groupings should do their utmost to ensure that their economic integration does not cause injury to, or otherwise adversely affect, the expansion of their imports from third countries, and, in particular, from developing countries, either individually or collectively.

10. "Regional economic groupings, integration or other forms of economic co-operation should be promoted among developing countries as a means of expanding their intra-regional and extra-regional trade and encouraging their economic growth and their industrial and agricultural diversification, with due regard to the special features of development of the various countries concerned, as well as their economic and social systems. It will be necessary to ensure that such co-operation makes an effective contribution to the economic development of these countries, and does not inhibit the economic development of other developing countries outside such groupings.

11. "International institutions and developed countries should provide an increasing net flow of international financial, technical and economic assistance to support and reinforce, by supplementing the export earnings of developing countries, the efforts made by them to accelerate their economic growth through diversification, industrialization and increase of productivity, on the basis of their national policies, plans and programmes of economic development. Such assistance should not be subject to any political or military conditions. This assistance, whatever its form and from whatever source, including foreign public and private loans and capital, should flow to developing countries on terms fully in keeping with their trade and development needs. International financial and monetary policies should be designed to take full account of the trade and development needs of developing countries.

12. "All countries recognize that a significant portion of resources released in successive stages as a result of the conclusion
of an agreement on general and complete disarmament under effective international control should be allocated to the promotion of
economic development in developing countries.

13. [The conference adopted by reference the proposals recommended by a separate UN group concerned with the special problems of land-locked countries. Basically these detailed proposals
called for the establishment of transit rights to the sea for such
nations. The text of the proposals can be found in the Official Rec
ords of the United Nations General Assembly, 19th Session, An-
nexes, Vol. 2 at pp. 67-71.]

14. "Complete decolonization, in compliance with the United
Nations Declaration on the Granting of Independence to Colonial
Countries and Peoples and the liquidation of the remnants of colonialism in all its forms, is a necessary condition for economic
development and the exercise of sovereign rights over natural
resources.

15. "The adoption of international policies and measures for
the economic development of the developing countries shall take
into account the individual characteristics and different stages of
development of the developing countries, special attention being
paid to the less developed among them, as an effective means of ensuring sustained growth with equitable opportunity for each developing country."

The special principles adopted in 1964 by the UN Conference
on Trade and Development outlined the moral obligations of industrial nations to cooperate with developing nations. Goals were
established to help expand the trade of developing nations, provide scientific, technical and financial assistance, train qualified
personnel, and increase imports of semi-manufactured and manufactured products from developing nations. Industrial nations were
to take measures to counteract the effects of substituting materials
for the primary commodities imported from developing nations.
Such measures included financial, technical and research assistance

to promote new applications for the displaced primary commodities.

The recommendations adopted by the conference refer to the obligation of developed nations not to manipulate prices of primary commodities in the international market but to stabilize them. Industrial nations were asked to aid the developing nations in establishing their own merchant shipping while guaranteeing the unrestricted use of existing transportation to carry goods and promote tourism. The special principles also proclaimed the right of developing nations to protect nascent industries since the industrialization and the modernization of agriculture are basic requirements for economic and social development.

Other special principles relate to methods of financial, scientific and technical assistance. In this respect the eleventh principle is of great importance. It establishes that bilateral or multilateral assistance to developing nations must be offered "in the form of grants or loans at the lowest possible interest rates, with long terms of payment and ample grace periods. The loans must not be conditional or in kind, particularly in the case of capital goods or technical assistance." According to this recommendation, credit and loans should be repaid in local currency or with primary commodities and industrial goods produced by debtor nations.

The first Trade and Development Conference apportioned the task of examining and discussing specific issues among five commissions. The first was assigned to study the international problems of primary commodities in light of three objectives: (a) to eliminate obstacles in the path of a rapid expansion of exports from developing nations to developed nations; (b) to promote the trade in primary commodities among developing nations; and (c) to conclude agreements to ensure stability of primary commodity prices at levels which were both equitable and remunerative.

The conference's second commission addressed its attention to the problems of manufactured and semi-manufactured goods with respect to three objectives: (a) to diversify and expand the exports of developing nations, (b) to provide them with easy access to the markets of developed nations, and (c) to increase trade in such products among the developing nations.

The third commission also had three tasks—analysis of the problems of promoting developing nations' commerce in "invisibles" (tourism and transportation), examination of the possibilities for compensatory financing to ensure price stability of primary commodity exports, and formulation of trade and aid policies hastening economic development.

The fourth commission studied international organizations and procedures governing world trade. It examined the need for eliminating duplicated effort and for coordinating and integrating of activities affecting international trade in order to serve the development needs of underdeveloped nations.

The fifth commission discussed possibilities for expanding international trade and its importance with respect to economic development.

The representatives of 120 member states assembled at UNCTAD I. In the course of the conference, the Group of 77 (so called because it first consisted of 77 developed nations) demonstrated great cohesiveness by voting as a group on all important issues. In spite of its practical limitations, the conference clearly stated the nature of the external and internal economic difficulties faced by developing nations. It publicized the serious problems caused by the impact of the great technological revolution on underdeveloped nations, and pointed out the adverse effects of the economic policies pursued by industrial nations. Also highlighted were the functional deficiencies of the existing means for international cooperation in regard to aid, trade, and development.

Without exaggeration it may be said that this conference was the first confrontation at the international level of the three groups of nations into which the world of the 1960s was divided: advanced capitalist nations, socialist countries, and a large bloc of developing nations comprised of the Group of 77, subsequently known as the Third World.

Following the conference, the UN General Assembly, by Resolution 1995 (adopted at the end of 1964) institutionalized the United Nations Conference on Trade and Development as an on-going body of the UN. It was to be directed by a Trade and Development Council with executive powers exercised by the representatives of 55 countries. (This was later expanded to 68 nations.) A general meeting would be held every four years. Its functions were summed up as follows:

1. Promote international trade, especially between nations in different stages of development, in order to advance economic development;

2. Formulate principles and policies on issues of international trade and economic development;

3. Formulate tactics to put these principles and policies into practice;

4. Review generally and help to coordinate the activities of other UN institutions with respect to international trade and economic development;

5. Promote the negotiation and adoption of multilateral trade instruments, and

6. Serve as a coordinating center for regional economic groups.

* * *

During the four years between the first and second general meetings of the conference, the economic relations between industrial and developing nations continued to deteriorate. The gap between the two steadily widened with respect to trade, savings and investment, foreign exchange, per capita production, and income. Resentment and frustration grew and the unfulfilled expectations stimulated by the First Conference served to arouse the feeling that it was imperative for developing nations to present a common front against the manipulations and policies of industrial nations.

Although the only source of unity stemmed from their common dependence vis-a-vis the centers of economic power, the developing nations decided to institutionalize the relationship begun at the first meeting held by the Group of 77. Ministerial-level representatives of these nations met in Algiers in October, 1967. This gathering produced the Algiers Charter in which Third World unity was proclaimed and a common policy regarding international trade and politics was announced.

The signatory nations of the Algiers Charter declared that in the early years of the 1960s exports from developing nations had continued to decline while exports from developed nations had increased and the price of some primary commodities had fallen. These factors reduced the purchasing power of Third World nations and aggravated their foreign debt problem. At the same time, developing nations were experiencing the effects of rapid population growth accompanying a backward technology and a relatively stagnant food production. The Algiers Charter pointed out that the promises in the final document of the first UN Conference on Trade and Development had failed to materialize. Accordingly, a seven-point plan of action was drafted.

The plan's first point recommended international negotiations and agreements for each primary commodity while stressing that efforts should be made to diversify production. Protective tariffs of the industrialized nations toward products of the Third World should be eliminated, but a preferential price system for products of the Third World should be established.

The second point suggested methods for increasing exports of manufactured and semi-manufactured goods from developing nations, for establishing a general preferential system for Third World products, for liberalizing the transfer of technology, and for increasing trade between nations with differing socio-economic systems.

The third point called for the adoption of specific methods for the flow of public and private international capital and urged the mobilization of the financial resources of Third World nations to meet the needs of development. Each nation resolved to participate in all negotiations and discussions regarding international monetary reform and the application of agreements on drawing rights from the International Monetary Fund.

The fourth point of the Algiers charter called attention to the need for a new international policy with regard to shipping, insurance, tourism, etc. It also suggested the revision of existing national legislation to promote merchant shipping, harbor improvements and tourism in developing nations.

The fifth and sixth points concerned matters of trade policies in general, the expansion of trade, and the economic integration of developing nations. Particular attention was given to the international division of labor, the transfer of technology, and the special problems of landlocked nations.

The final point focused on special measures for further development in the most underdeveloped nations of the Third World.

At its Algiers meeting the Group of 77 also decided to become a permanent body and to meet before each UNCTAD general session whenever the need arose.

The influence of the Algiers Charter became evident when the agenda adopted for the second UN Conference on Trade and Development (held in New Delhi, India) turned out to be almost identical to the plan of action proposed by the Algiers Charter.

* * *

The second UNCTAD conference was held in New Delhi during February and March of 1968. In keeping with the program set forth by the first conference and the Algiers Charter, the main issues discussed were: trade of primary commodities, promotion of trade among developing nations, promotion of exports of Third World manufactured and semi-processed goods, and international financing.

In regard to primary commodities, the New Delhi conference adopted resolutions designed to increase the production and trade of cacao, sugar, oils, rubber, hard fibers, and jute. It recommended that international meetings be held for the purpose of negotiating agreements relating to trade and price stability of sugar and cacao. It asked the Commission for Basic Commodities to suggest measures for a general basic commodities agreement. A special study of "a minimum agricultural income" was undertaken.

To further the principle of non-reciprocal trade for Third World nations a Commission on Preferences was established to assist the UN Trade and Development Council. A major objective of the commission was to review the application of a generalized system of preferences in the light of special conditions and problems of the most underdeveloped nations.

Developed nations were asked to transfer annually to developing countries financial resources amounting to a net value of at least one percent of the industrial nation's gross national product—i.e., at least 80% of this sum in the form of grants or a minimum of 90% as grants or loans with an interest rate no higher than 2.5% and a minimum payment term of 30 years, with minimum grace periods of eight years. The conference also recommended that the industrial production of developing nations be accepted as re-payment of loans and suggested that restrictions and "conditional loans" be eliminated. It was agreed that developing nations should mobilize their entire internal resources to hasten and expedite development.

The New Delhi conference suggested general rules to promote foreign private investments in developing nations, and agreed to study the possibility of creating regional development funds. The Third World's desire for more liberal criteria in the operation of the International Monetary Fund was emphasized. In addition, consideration was given to the creation of a supplementary financing fund for nations whose development plans were affected by a decline in income from exports.

The conference also recommended reduction of the cost of in-surance and reinsurance in developing nations and an arrangement under which at least some premiums would be invested in Third World nations. Other recommendations called for the creation of a system of consultation on merchant shipping and representation of the national companies of developing countries at shipping con-ferences of international organizations. The development of Third World merchant shipping, the promotion of tourism, and the special problems of landlocked nations were also considered. It was agreed that so far as possible international organizations should adopt special provisions in favor of the least developed Third World countries.

Despite the meagerness of concrete results, the first two UN Conferences on Trade and Development proved suitable international forums in which to analyze and propose solutions for the problems of underdevelopment. The fact that many of these solutions have not been applied is due not only to the failure of the developed nations to cooperate but also to the increasingly bureaucratic character of the conferences. However, UNCTAD remained virtually the only institution which allowed the international community to debate and try to resolve the complicated problems of economic relations among poor and rich nations.

The establishment of UNCTAD was a great step forward from the situation prior to 1964, when trade and development problems were treated individually through multilateral organizations or bilateral agreements—a situation exceedingly disadvantageous for underdeveloped nations.

5: The Charter of Economic
Rights Takes Shape

The third United Nations Conference on Trade and Development (UNCTAD III) held in Santiago in 1972 reflected the cumulative experience of eight years of unsuccessful efforts to redress the imbalance in international economic relations—a situation that unfortunately created an atmosphere of marked pessimism. Moreover, the attitude of the industrial nations in 1972 was less amenable to concessions than it had been at the previous UNCTAD meetings.

The "Group of 77" (which had been expanded to include 96 nations) met in Lima, Peru, in 1971, with the purpose of presenting a common front at the forthcoming Santiago conference. That purpose was not achieved for three main reasons. First, there were great differences in the levels of development among the three large geographic blocs (Asia, Africa, and Latin America) as well as among nations within those blocs. The second reason was the manipulation practiced by some industrial nations, especially former colonial powers. Finally, and this was perhaps the most important, distrust prevailed because of the international monetary crisis that resulted in the suspension in August, 1971, of the international convertibility of the United States dollar into gold.

Nevertheless, some remnants of unity were evident at Santiago. The greatest solidarity among the Third World nations arose out of antagonism toward the United States as a result of its unilateral action to restore its balance of payments. This action seriously diminished the purchasing power of many developing nations. Dollar devaluation made foreign aid less valuable; trade preferences to developing nations were less useful, and open hostility was shown toward the international agreement on coffee and a similar draft agreement on cacao.

The countries of the European Common Market and Great Britain were bitterly criticized for their niggardly foreign assistance policies and trade restrictions. In addition, there was resentment toward the industrialized socialist nations which had not lived up to their commitments. Though development aid from socialist countries to Third World nations had doubled in the 1960s, it remained insignificant. Moreover, socialist countries continued to impose restrictions on imports of primary commodities.

At the New Delhi conference many industrial nations had voted to grant aid to developing nations of at least one per cent of their gross national products. This would have been a great net increase in aid. Such aid, according to data of the industrial nations, had doubled from seven billion to 14.2 billion dollars. But the nature of the aid had changed; it included not only export credits granted by the industrial nations to the developing nations but also private foreign investments. Objectively these investments should not be considered aid; they are purely and simply business deals, often of a dubious nature. In 1970 the nearly 100 nations constituting the Third World received 7.8 billion dollars in governmentally supplied aid through bilateral or multilateral institutional arrangements. The remainder of the official amount (6.4 billion dollars) consisted of direct private investments and export credits which were conditional in the majority of cases. Thus the percentage of foreign aid actually decreased between 1960 and 1970.

The third UN Conference on Trade and Development opened its sessions on April 13, 1972. The intended nature of the conference was recognized in the welcoming speech by the President of Chile, Dr. Salvador Allende, who reminded the delegates that they had "been called to rectify an unjust division of labor, based on an inhuman concept of man."

As at the two previous conferences, the nations grouped them-

selves into three blocs—Soviet bloc, U.S.-NATO bloc, and others—
with much less cohesion. In fact, the international monetary
crisis and the political tension between East and West led to more
or less fixed positions that rendered general agreement on essential issues impossible. This same lack of cohesion was also evident among the developing nations. In consequence, despite their
resentment toward the developed nations, the likelihood of presenting a common Third World viewpoint was very remote.

The official agenda included the subjects which had become
traditional—primary commodities, manufactured and semi-manufactured goods, financial aid to developing countries, trade relations between nations of different socio-economic systems, economic
integration of developed nations, problems of shipping, insurance,
and tourism, and preferential measures in favor of the most underdeveloped nations. This time, however, other subjects were added
—for example, the repercussions of the international monetary
crisis, the problems relating to the resources from the sea, the
economic effects of disarmament, the economic consequences of
the closing of the Suez Canal, and reform of international economic organizations.

Apart from UNCTAD, but parallel to its goals, a group of 24
developing nations had met in Caracas in April, 1972, to discuss
monetary reform. They approved resolutions urging increased
representation of the developing world in the International Monetary Fund and establishment of a group to study monetary reform
consisting of 20 nations of which nine would be developing nations.

The UN conference in Santiago organized its work into six principal commissions and three task forces. The first commission
appraised problems and policies affecting primary commodities;
the second addressed itself to manufactured and semi-manufactured goods; the third examined the repercussions of the international monetary situation on international trade and development (especially its effect on developing nations), and problems
related to financial resources for development. The fourth com-

mission tackled problems with respect to shipping insurance, and tourism. The fifth dealt with trade relations between nations with different economic and social systems, and the sixth studied special measures to assist the most underdeveloped nations. The three task forces were directed to study the institutional arrangements of UNCTAD, the expansion of trade, and problems of the transfer of technology.

Some issues were presented directly to the conference's plenary session. Of the proposed resolutions considered during working sessions, two were of major importance. The first dealt with the desire of developing nations to participate in the forthcoming international negotiations on the General Agreement on Tariffs and Trade (GATT). The second involved preparation of a charter on the Economic Rights and Duties of States and was based on a draft prepared by the "Group of 77" and inspired by a speech of Dr. Luis Echeverria delivered at the plenary session of the conference on April 19, 1972.

Dr. Echeverria's proposal was significant for several reasons. It summarized the expectations of the Third World nations and their just demands on industrial nations; second, it revived the common desire to consolidate the fragmented unity of the "Group of 77" — as evidenced by the enthusiasm with which the proposed resolution on the charter was greeted by the Third World nations. The concept itself, and later the draft charter, were historically opportune in light of the need precipitated by the international monetary crisis to formulate rules by which international economic relations should be conducted.

The nature of the confrontation between developing and developed nations and the importance attached to this confrontation by the industrial nations are evident in the speech by Dr. S. Mansholt, former President of the European Common Market, at the opening of a conference on the industrial policy of the Market. Dr. Mansholt called attention to three significant factors— the deep frustration and growing anger of the Third World nations toward the economic and financial policies of the developed nations, the failure of the first development decade, and the widening gap between the rich and poor nations. He concluded that the developed world was doing nothing to help the developing nations.

It became markedly evident that there was no alternative but to begin thinking and acting purposefully to solve the current world crisis rationally and in a spirit of frank international cooperation. The Charter of Economic Rights and Duties of States provided a statement of principles upon which the new international order could be based.

*　　*　　*

In addressing the United Nations General Assembly in 1971, Dr. Echeverria pointed out that although the East-West cold war was diminishing, it was being supplanted by a worldwide conflict even more disquieting—that between rich and poor nations. The only way to avoid the perils of this conflict, he warned, was through reliance on reason and the rule of law:

"Frustration and reaction against unfair treatment must be prevented from provoking a new and radical schism . . . between the affluent nations and those struggling to surmount under-development . . . there will be no peace in the world until there has been a basic reorganization of economic relations among nations. Today, the threat of atomic war is as serious as that of the growing inequality between the rich countries and the poor . . . [Therefore] we must fight for an era of economic, social, and political equality, and we must break the bonds of servitude, so that all peoples may fulfill their creative potentials. We must guide along peaceful paths the just aspirations for freedom, health, food, housing, education, and full employment." (The complete text of Dr. Echeverria's speech appears in the appendix of this book.)

It was against this as background that Dr. Echeverria spoke to the delegates at the third United Nations Conference on Trade and Development in 1972. "The progress of mankind as of this moment is indivisible," he declared in a notable passage. "Events in each country affect all the others, and condition their evolution. To view the future in purely local terms is to ignore the international character of the present-day economy. No community can fully resolve its problems without considering them from a general perspective."

The nature of the existing gap between the rich and poor nations acquired new significance from this viewpoint. It was clearly necessary to seek common points of interest among the nations sharing the same planet. Economic distribution must be based upon morality rather than strength: "where there is inequality [of bargaining power] there cannot be equal treatment."

The existing system of international economic relations, Dr. Echeverria asserted, was institutionalized in favor of the strongest nations. "The centers of world power impose trade conditions upon the rest of the world. They also weaken the capacity for action of lesser-developed countries, opposing essential structural changes, or intervening in their political processes." Moreover, the strongest nations were transferring their employment and productivity problems to the developing nations while ignoring the poverty in which two-thirds of humanity lived.

All too often, Dr. Echeverria declared, commitments which the developed nations made to the developing ones have not been kept. Many industrial nations have returned to protectionist trade policies, worsening already unfavorable balances of trade by the nations producing primary commodities. Therefore the gap between developed and developing nations continues to widen. The terms of trade for important products have deteriorated; industrial nations are flooding the market with surplus goods; the economically more advanced nations spend relatively less of their gross national expenditures on materials from the less-developed nations, and the developing nations which were intended to benefit from foreign lending find the foreign debt load hard to bear.

Postponements of trade preferences previously agreed upon, Dr. Echeverria added, further aggravated the trade problems of the less-developed nations, which in turn generated dangerous political and social reactions. "Our nations view with disappointment the fact that the air at international forums is filled with words that are rarely followed by actions . . . It is useless for us to waste our time asking for what others are unwilling to give, in reaching precarious agreements, and feeling sorry later because such promises are broken."

Dr. Echeverria warned that the situation was exacerbated by the developing nations' population growth. Since their population was likely to double within 30 years, it would take an enormous effort for mankind to double its economic production within the same period. "The rate of population growth must be reduced, because it is expedient for our people; but the main task before us is to stimulate a vigorous and integrated [economic] development."

In regard to international financial problems, Dr. Echeverria stressed the need for greater Third World participation in the Industrial Monetary Fund. He urged a "democratization" of the Fund to enable developing nations to participate in true equality with the developed nations. "We are not here to negotiate with industrial nations for advantages to benefit the economic oligarchies of the underdeveloped world; we are searching for a propitious framework within which to bring about the political, cultural, technological and social progress of our people."

One of the most acute problems facing developing countries stems from their backward technology. Since technological advancement depends not only on scientific knowledge but also on sizeable investments the majority of the Third World nations do not have the ability to develop a technology remotely capable of competing with that of industrial nations. Thus the acquisition of technological know-how from industrial nations by developing nations is a matter of great importance.

Closely linked to the transfer of technology financing is the role played by direct foreign investments. When those who make such investments, Dr. Echeverria declared, do not share responsibility with national entrepreneurs or provide for the transfer of technological innovations without taking into account the benefits derived from foreign markets, the investments become only an extension of the old forms of colonialism. It is for this reason that foreign investments must be subject to the laws and goals of the host nations. Unfortunately, industrial nations have all too often used legal disputes of dubious merit to intervene in the internal affairs of developing nations even though this flagrantly violated international law.

In alluding to Article 27 of the Mexican Constitution, Dr. Echeverria stated: "Every nation must recognize and honor the right of every other to dispose freely of its natural resources without any outside pressure or interference. For their part, multinational corporations must abstain from intervening directly or indirectly in matters which pertain only to the sovereign decision-making process of each nation."

Since some of the most important natural resources lie under the seas, and because sea fauna is a valuable food source, the judicious yet optimum exploitation of the seas is, Dr. Echeverria reasoned, "an imperative of our time." Accordingly, Mexico would strive "to obtain [international] legal recognition of a patrimonial sea extending 200 miles offshore, in which the coastal state would unquestionably exercise exclusive and preferential fishing rights as well as general rights over all economic resources."

In the course of his wide-ranging speech Dr. Echeverria charged that the developed nations were largely responsible for the ecological deterioration of the planet; hence it was their "duty . . . to adopt the necessary research and economic policies to correct the present situation" but he cautioned that concern over pollution not be used as an excuse to block the material progress of the developing nations.

Dr. Echeverria also appealed for international unity in the formulation of "duties and rights for the protection of the weak nations" based on equity and fairness. "Let us," he declared, "separate economic cooperation from the sphere of good will and let us place it in the sphere of law. Let us transfer the principles of solidarity among men to the area of relations between nations."

Dr. Echeverria urged recognition of the following basic principles:

"Freedom [for each nation] to dispose at will of its natural resources.

"Respect for each nation's absolute right to adopt the economic structure it deems most suitable, and to impose upon private property the requirements that the public interest dictates.

"Renunciation of the use of methods and economic pressures which reduce the political sovereignty of nations.

"Subordination of foreign capital to the laws of the host nation.

"Express prohibition against intervention by multinational corporations in the internal affairs of nations.

"Abolition of commercial practices which discriminate against the exports of non-industrial nations."

"[Granting of international] economic preferences proportional with the level of development.

"Agreements which guarantee the stability and fair price of primary commodities.

"Ample and adequate transfer of scientific and technological advances at the lowest cost and as rapidly as possible to the most underdeveloped nations.

"Allocation of greater resources to long-term development financing with no conditions attached and at low interest rates."

6: Mexico Points the Way

Mexico's international policy has long been characterized by adherence to the tenets of international law. It has striven to inculcate respect for the principles of nonintervention, of self-determination, of juridical equality of states, of peaceful settlement of disputes, and of cooperation among members of the international community.

In recent years Mexico has maintained an independent posture toward its powerful northern neighbor—an independence expressed, for example, in Mexico's unwillingness to sever relations with Cuba, to countenence Cuba's expulsion from the Organization of American States, and to broaden the military role of Pan-Americanism. In the United Nations, Mexico was one of the first countries to insist that of the "two Chinas" only the People's Republic of China should be represented. Though Mexico expressed reservations as to the procedure by which the Assembly voted on the question, it subsequently affirmed its position by establishing diplomatic relations with Peking. Moreover, Mexico played a major role in proscribing nuclear weapons through its support of the Treaty of Tlatelolco.

* * *

Some leaders fail because they are too far ahead or behind their times. Men who are ahead of their time are invariably misunderstood by their contemporaries and do not adapt to prevalent conditions. Men who live behind their time generally hanker for earlier eras because they are unable to understand or accept contemporary conditions. The speed with which events now succeed each other, the rate at which social change takes place, and the very depth of such change almost render obsolete what seemed sacred and immutable yesterday.

Men of their time possess a quality which enables them to perceive current problems, interpret them incisively, and deal with them realistically. A man of his time, unlike men who live in the past, is always concerned with the present and its impact on the future. He strives for betterment of man's lot here and now. Dr. Luis Echeverria is such a man.

Dr. Echeverria became the President of Mexico in 1971 at a critical point of history when the affairs of his country and the international situation required bold innovative action. Conscious of the challenges posed by the 1970's, he became convinced that Mexico could and should play a dynamic role as a member of the international community and as a nation of the emerging Third World.

In a speech Dr. Echeverria delivered before Mexico's legislature on February 21, 1973, prior to setting out on a trip across three continents, he declared: "Mexico does not wish to be a passive spectator of history. We do not accept the fact that the new configuration of the world revolves exlcusively around the great centers of power, without the participation of countries such as ours, which do not aspire to any form of domination, but only to the well-being of their people, the improvement of their living conditions and the pursuit of progress in peace and freedom." These words clearly indicate the nature of Dr. Echeverria's deep concern about world affairs and the importance which he attaches to them.

Dr. Echeverria realizes, of course, that the foreign policy of a nation is and should be an extension of its domestic policy. It was with this in mind that he launched his battle to redeem the inalienable rights of developing nations and became a leader of the Third World.

*   *   *

Some of Dr. Echeverria's most important ideas are rooted in the ideals of the Mexican Revolution, which had scarcely subsided during his boyhood. The ideology of that revolution, like that of Mexico's present government, is nationalistic, egalitarian, and anti-imperialistic. This revolution, the last of the nineteenth century style liberal democratic revolutions, can be considered the first true social revolution of the twentieth century. Some of its central ideas are inherent in the Charter of Economic Rights and Duties of States.

Throughout Mexico's history, its people have deeply resented the plundering of their natural resources by colonial powers. It is because of such exploitation (particularly during the dictatorship of Porfirio Diaz) that Article 27 of the Mexican Constitution states unequivocally: "The ownership of land and sea within the national boundaries is vested originally in the nation." Unconditional sovereignty is a primary tenet in Dr. Echeverria's thinking; it was uppermost in his mind when he declared, "Regardless of how dire our need for financial and technological resources might be, we must never place the patrimony and future of Mexico at the mercy of interests which are not our own."

*   *   *

Dr. Echeverria's historic proposal at the United Nations Conference on Trade and Development in 1972 must be viewed in broad perspective, but it would be a mistake to overlook his personal commitment to it and why he became the main champion of the Charter of Economic Rights and Duties of States finally adopted by the United Nations in 1974.

Soon after Dr. Echeverria was elected Mexico's President, the role of his country in world affairs took on a truly dynamic character. His earliest actions included the appointment of missions to Canada, Europe, and Japan authorized to promote technical and financial cooperation. Simultaneously he intensified Mexico's ties to Latin America by meeting with the heads of state of Guatemala, Costa Rica, and Nicaragua during the summer of 1971.

International affairs occupied a prominent place in Dr. Echeverria's state of the union address. This message stressed Mexico's advocacy of world disarmament and the enormous stake the smaller nations have in the maintenance of peace.

President Echeverria's speech on October 5, 1971 before the United Nations General Assembly, in which he urged greater equality of nations based on a just economic order, was a further logical step. The defense of the interests of the Third World against those of industrial nations was a central theme of his address. No country, no matter how small, could afford to remain uninvolved in international decision-making processes. Thus Mexico clearly aligned itself with the oppressed nations of the world.

After making his historic proposal of April 19, 1972—i.e., his proposal for the formulation of the Charter of Economic Rights and Duties of States—Dr. Echeverria set about enlisting support for it among the leaders of Third World nations. The first to join hands with him was the President of Chile, Dr. Salvador Allende. A declaration signed by Dr. Allende on April 21 stated: "The President of Chile approves and supports the initiative taken by the President of Mexico in his speech calling for the preparation of a Charter of Economic Rights and Duties of States as a legal code embodying principles which will regulate international economic relations within a framework of justice."

The success of the charter proposal did not depend solely on the backing of nations facing circumstances similar to those of Mexico. It was also necessary to enlist the support of nations with different economic conditions. Aware of the enormous importance of obtaining the backing of socialist nations and of the fact that some industrial nations were unlikely to support the charter, Dr. Echeverria visited China and the Soviet Union as well as Canada, England, France, and Belgium in the Spring of 1973.

Dr. Echeverria secured Canada's support for the concept of the charter as well as backing for the Treaty of Tlatelolco banning nuclear weapons. During his trips to England, Belgium, and France —highly industrialized nations which benefit from the inequitable world economic order—he urged their leaders to recognize and fulfill their obligations to the developing Third World nations. The leaders with whom he met promised to study the charter and indicated they would support some aspects of it but later their countries voted against it at the United Nations General Assembly. Rich nations do not, of course, easily relinquish the privileges they enjoy. Since, however, the charter offers substantial advantages to industrial nations, Dr. Echeverria feels confident that they will eventually recognize its value.

The Soviet Union and China became early backers of the charter proposal and as a result it came to enjoy the support of two of the three blocs in which the nations of the world tend to be grouped. Significantly, Russia, China, and Rumania were the main allies of the Group of 77 in the United Nations General Assembly that approved the document. In a report to the Mexican people in September, 1973, Dr. Echeverria declared: "The nations I visited are a major part of the world's contemporary political and economic experience. We are not prejudiced, nor are we afraid of imaginary influences. We accept ideological pluralism as the necessary characteristic of our time. On the basis of a broader viewpoint, we reassert our confidence in ourselves and in the path we have taken."

In February, 1974, Dr. Echeverria again set out on official visits, this time to the Pope and the headquarters of the international organizations concerned with atomic energy, industrial development, and food. While in Europe he warned: "We must convince the great powers that it is to their advantage to cooperate with the Third World. This is a difficult task . . . but international stability requires us to persevere."

At a Salzburg meeting of heads of state held under the auspices of the Club of Rome, Dr. Echeverria presented a humanistic viewpoint which differed markedly with the pessimistic speculations of the technocratic nations represented in the Club:

"Apart from the dubious scientific value of recent gloomy studies . . . there is an obvious failure to take into account philosophical and political considerations relating to the causes and consequences of the present situation. These studies virtually correspond to an ideological attitude and the proposed alternatives reflect views of dominant groups which desire to absolve themselves from objective responsibility for the nature and solution of our problems . . . It is inadmissible to permit the alternatives to be viewed from the economic and political perspective of powerful nations largely to blame for the extravagance and colonialism which created the situation they are alarmed about today . . . It is unfair to expect the societies of the Third World to subsidize, in effect, the prosperity only a few opulent societies enjoy.

"The catastrophic vision of the future that has been predicted is a notion of the industrial nations we cannot accept . . . The true limitations of growth are moral and political . . . It is imperative that new frontiers of humanity be established through a fundamental change in the relationships among social classes, nations, and groups of nations."

In taking the position that technocratic answers serve the interests of those who sponsor them, Dr. Echeverria underscored the inequities of the existing international economic system: "The present structure of the world presupposes an international division of labor that is unacceptable". One of the most disturbing trends of our time has been the rise of multinational corporations which mock the jurisdictions of nations. A basic requirement for ensuring the growth of developing nations, he continued, is restriction of the operations of such corporations by means of "regulations taking into full account the correlation between their power and their responsibilities to host nations."

While stressing the need for foreign investment, Dr. Echeverria contended that it too must be controlled. "Foreign investment," he stated, "is welcome as long as it improves the technology of developing nations, promotes new and dynamic industries, contributes to the fulfillment of national goals, and encourages exports to all of the world's nations. Unfortunately foreign investment often tends to overlook these considerations."

"I am convinced," Dr. Echeverria declared, "that only with respect for the autonomous will of the people, for their political institutions, for their cultural values, for their social well being, can stability and peace be attained . . . Cooperation in the economic and political spheres must not be used to perpetuate the old colonial boundaries or spheres of influence . . . The world is now radically different than it was a quarter of a century ago. No nation or group of nations, however powerful, should be allowed to dominate world affairs . . . The exploitation of weak nations by powerful ones must be stopped. A more equitable international order such as that envisioned by the Charter of Economic Rights and Duties of States is clearly imperative."

During his trip to Rome in 1974, Dr. Echeverria obtained for the charter the support in principle of Italy's President, Giovanni Leone, and he visited Pope Paul VI for the purpose of thanking him for encouraging some of the charter's central ideas.

In 1974, during a trip to five Latin American countries—Ecuador, Peru, Argentina, Brazil, and Venezuela—Dr. Echeverria spoke out loud and clear for hemisphere solidarity and he proposed a series of practical measures designed to hasten economic development in this part of the world. He urged, for example, the creation of multinational Latin American corporations to counter the operations of huge foreign corporations.

In addressing the United Nations Third Conference on the Law of the Sea, held in Carcas in July, 1974, Dr. Echeverria called upon the delegates to "guarantee the utilization . . . of the sea and its resources for the benefit of all nations, instead of only a few." This is one of the main objectives of the Charter of Economic Rights and Duties of States.

At the United Nations Conference on Resources and the Environment held in Stockholm, Mexico's representatives expressed Dr. Echeverria's conviction that the earth's resources should be conserved and protected for fulfillment, not reduction of man's needs but the delegates from the industrial nations persisted in diverting attention from the main reason for ecological deterioration: wasteful consumption by rich nations.

At the World Population Conference held in Bucharest in September, 1974, the head of Mexico's delegation, Dr. Mario Moya Palencia, affirmed the need for the Charter of Economic Rights and Duties of States conceived by Dr. Echeverria. "We would progress very slowly towards a rational world population," he pointed out, "if we are unable to achieve a rational world economy . . . Approval of the charter by the United Nations will be the best contribution to the goal of this conference—improvement of the quality of life of all men." Significantly, the conference approved a resolution supporting the charter. This action was especially gratifying because the resolution was adopted by consensus with no objection raised by the industrial nations.

Several weeks later, in October, the charter figured prominently in discussions between Dr. Echeverria and President Gerald Ford at the White House. Unfortunately the United States remained partial to the interests of its multinational corporations and voted against the charter when it came before the United Nations General Assembly.

A month before the Assembly's meeting, Dr. Echeverria was a prominent participant at the World Food Conference held in Rome. In an address at this forum that attracted wide attention he spoke out forcefully against the policies of powerful nations which have been injurious to the developing nations and have contributed "to the hunger of humanity and the destruction of mankind's natural resources."

Throughout the past few years Dr. Echeverria has emerged not only as a spokesman of the developing nations but also as a leader of people everywhere who have come to realize that the world must face up to its problems realistically, humanely, and promptly.

7: United Nations Action

Thirty-two months passed between April 19, 1972, when President Echeverria proposed his idea for the Charter of Economic Rights and Duties of States, and December 12, 1974, when it was finally approved by the General Assembly of the United Nations. During this period the Group of 40 nations that had been entrusted with the preparation of the charter held four sessions, the last and most fruitful of which took place in Tlatelolco, Mexico.

In this chapter we take a brief look at the process by which the Group of 40 prepared the charter and we examine the vicissitudes and antagonisms surrounding it and its evolution until its approval by an overwhelming majority in the United Nations General Assembly in 1974. (The full text of the charter appears in the next chapter.)

The significance of Dr. Echeverria's proposal before the third United Nations Conference on Trade and Development in Santiago on April 19, 1972, was promptly realized by the representatives of the participating nations. His contribution was not just another speech on subjects more or less within the limits of the conference agenda but an urgent appeal to the international community to recognize the symptoms and causes of the critical problems confronting the postwar world.

Dr. Echeverria's proposal summarized the demands and expectations of the Third World nations. In its formulation of rights and duties it expressed the need to establish a new international economic order realistically reflecting present-day conditions as well as the aspirations of the majority of mankind. The proposal offered concrete guidelines for regulations governing the relations among all nations, irrespective of their levels of development or their political systems, with the purpose of harmonizing their differences in the interests of international cooperation and security.

The impact of Dr. Echeverria's speech was considerable—so much so that delegates at the conference decided to include his proposal in one of their resolutions. Representatives of the various nations, especially the Group of 77, contributed their ideas and formulated a draft that was passed by the conference's plenary session. This was the origin of Resolution 45, which formally began the process by which the Charter of Economic Rights and Duties of States was eventually agreed upon by the international community.

Resolution 45 was approved by a vote of 90 in favor, none against, with 19 abstentions by countries which, without denying the importance of the draft, believed there had been too little time to consider it. The nations which approved the resolution consisted of the entire Group of 77, the socialist nations and some industrial nations with market economies—notably France, Belgium, and the Netherlands.

The preamble of Resolution 45 gave cognizance to "the urgent need in the international community to establish generally accepted norms to govern international economic relations systematically . . ." The main body of the resolution takes note of Dr. Echeverria's proposal and:

"1. Decides to establish a Working Group composed of government representatives of thirty-one member States to draw up the text of a draft charter. The Working Group shall be appointed as soon as possible by the Secretary-General of UNCTAD in consultation with States which are members of the Conference;

"2. Decides that the Working Group shall use as basic elements in its work:

"(a) The general, special and other principles as approved by the Conference at its first session;

"(b) Any proposals or suggestions on the subject made during the third session of the Conference;

"(c) All documents mentioned above and other relevant resolutions adopted within the framework of the United Nations, particularly the International Development Strategy for the Second United Nations Development Decade;

"(d) The principles contained in the Charter of Algiers and the Declaration and Principles of the Action Programme of Lima;

"3. Further decides that the draft prepared by the Working Group shall be sent to States which are members of UNCTAD in order that they can communicate their suggestions, it being understood that the Working Group shall reconvene to elaborate the draft charter further in the light of comments and suggestions to be received from governments of member States;

"4. Recommends to the Trade and Development Board that it examine, as a matter of priority, at its thirteenth session, the report of the above-mentioned Working Group, and the comments and suggestions made by States members of UNCTAD, and transmit that report, with its comments, to the General Assembly at its twenty-eighth session;

"5. Invites the General Assembly upon receipt of the above-mentioned report of the Trade and Development Board, and the views expressed by the governments during the consideration of the item in the General Assembly, to decide upon the opportunity and procedure for the drafting and adoption of the charter."

It is especially significant that Resolution 45 emphasized the importance of Dr. Echeverria's proposal, the conviction that the charter be the result of cooperation by all nations representing every ideology and all political systems, the desire to draw on previous experiences of the United Nations (especially the experiences of the trade and development conferences held in Geneva and New Delhi), and the emphasis placed on the need to adopt the charter promptly in order to mitigate the desperate plight of many of the developing nations.

The United Nations General Assembly examined the report of UNCTAD III on December 19, 1972. Indicative of the intense interest expressed in Resolution 45 regarding the Charter of Economic Rights and Duties of States was the decision to enlarge, from

31 to 40 nations, "the composition of the Working Group established to draw up the text of a draft charter of the economic rights and duties of states . . ." (UN Resolution 3037). This is the origin of the Group of 40 entrusted with preparing the draft charter. The group met on four occasions, three times in Geneva and the last time in Mexico City, before presenting its draft to the United Nations Economic and Social Council.

The developing nations of the Group of 77, who constituted a majority, were in a position to obtain approval of their own draft by the United Nations General Assembly at its 1973 session but they preferred not to press their advantage, and accepted delay for another year in the hope of securing an understanding with the industrial nations, and thereby achieve a charter reflecting the interests of all nations, rich and poor alike. Thus United Nations Resolution 3082 extended the mandate of the working group, stipulated that the Group of 40 meet at two separate sessions during 1974, and reaffirmed the need to adopt the charter "to establish or improve norms of universal application for the development of international economic relations on a just and equitable basis."

The resolution also reaffirmed the desire to bring the charter under discussion as soon as possible and be included in the agenda of the General Assembly's next session.

President Echeverria's efforts in behalf of the charter's adoption and his concern over the slow-moving manner in which its preparation was proceeding cannot be disregarded. Three months before the 1973 General Assembly, he expressed his concern in a message to Kurt Waldheim, the Secretary-General of the United Nations, in which he asked that UN procedures be altered in order to hasten the charter's approval.

When the Group of 40 met for the third time during February 1974, it debated the various drafts of the charter paragraph by paragraph. At times there were as many as nine different versions of some proposed provisions. The progress made in the course of these debates was on the whole satisfactory. Full agreement was reached on most of the preamble, which stressed that "the fundamental purpose of this charter [is] to promote *just and equitable* economic relations between nations."

All the participants in the Group of 40 also agreed on Chapter I of the charter, which spelled out the fundamental principles for the regulation of international economic relations. The most important of these principles dealt with national sovereignty, territorial integrity, political independence of states, sovereign equality, non-aggression, non-intervention, equal rights and self-determination of peoples, the peaceful settlement of disputes, and respect for human rights and fundamental freedoms. Chapter I provoked only minor differences of opinion, often semantic ones.

The Group of 40 was composed of both great powers and small nations representing all manner of economic systems. They included:

Australia	Egypt	Japan	Rumania
Belgium	France	Kenya	Soviet Union
Bolivia	Guatemala	Mexico	Spain
Brazil	Hungary	Morocco	Sri Lanka
Bulgaria	India	Netherlands	United Kingdom
Canada	Indonesia	Nigeria	United States
Chile	Iraq	Pakistan	West Germany
China	Italy	Peru	Yugoslavia
Czechoslovakia	Ivory Coast	Philippines	Zaire
Denmark	Jamaica	Poland	Zambia

Since the proposal to be considered by these nations was Mexican in origin, Dr. Jorge Castenada, Mexico's representative to the international organizations located in Geneva and a distinguished expert on international affairs, was elected chairman of the group.

The first meeting took place in Geneva at the United Nations Palace between February 12 and 23, 1973. At the very outset the delegates recognized that the document they were drafting should "contribute to the achievement of a more rational and just economic order through the reorganization of economic cooperation for the protection of weaker nations." The result of the first meeting was the adoption of an outline of the juridical content of the Charter of Economic Rights and Duties of States.

The group's second meeting took place in Geneva between July

16 and 27, 1973. This was expected to be the last meeting but antagonisms that arose prevented agreement on anything but a portion of the preamble and a few sections of the charter's text. Although alternative drafts were offered by delegates from Third World nations, objections raised by representatives of the industrial countries made it impossible to reconcile all viewpoints. Debate was especially heated over the content of the charter's second chapter.

Among the most important paragraphs on which agreement was reached were those appearing in the final text as Articles 1 and 9. These affirmed the sovereign right of every state to freely choose its economic system and the responsibility of all states "to cooperate in the economic, social, cultural, scientific and technological fields for the promotion of economic and social progress throughout the world, especially that of the developing nations."

The third meeting of the Group of 40 was held in Geneva February 4 to 22, 1974. At its end many issues remained unsettled. The difference in outlook on some topics was very great. In the case of the second paragraph of Chapter II of the proposed charter, for example, there were eight different drafts. One draft of this paragraph proposed by the Group of 77 declared: "It is the inalienable right of each State to exercise freely, full and permanent sovereignty over its entire wealth and natural resources, thus being able to dispose of them freely and fully . . . . This right includes nationalization of foreign property . . . . *Each State has the right to determine the appropriate amount owed as compensations, as well as the method of payment . . . . Any dispute on the matter will be settled by its tribunals under the domestic law of the nationalizing State.*" [italics added]

The Third World nations obviously felt that there is no higher judge of a nation's internal actions than that nation's own government. On the other hand, the text prepared by the European Economic Community in draft four said:

"Each State enjoys a permanent sovereignty over its natural

resources which must be exercised for the well-being of the people and the economic development of the nation.

"To promote the national interest, security and wealth, *States with natural resources have a right to dispose of them which also includes nationalization* . . . *These rights must be exercised in conjunction with the pertinent provisions in international law, particularly with regard to the payment of a prompt, sufficient and effective idemnity to the dispossessed owners.* [Emphasis added]

"In the exercise of national sovereignty . . . . the exigencies and interdependent nature of the economies of all states must be taken into account, as well as the need to contribute to the balanced expansion of the world economy."

The United States draft on the same matter took the following position: "Within the framework of international law, all states have the right to dispose freely and fully of their natural resources in order to promote the well-being of their people and further their economic development . . . *Appropriate compensation for nationalization must be paid with reference to international law* and according to the national law of the state which adopts such measures in the full exercise of its sovereignty." [Emphasis added]

The differences reflected by the various drafts were fundamental. To determine procedures for the nationalization of resources and the amount of indemnity due in accordance with the rules of national law is one thing; to determine them according to international law is quite another. The former interpretation means that each country may determine, in the full exercise of its sovereignty, questions of compensation according to its own law, whereas the latter means that the decision is up to the big powers.

It must not be forgotten that international law is fundamentally the law of an oligarchy in which the more powerful nations enjoy dominant influence. One of the best examples of this is the so-called "veto right" which the great powers rely on in the United Nations Security Council. Thus, to accept the notion that nationalization and indemnity should be subject to international law is equivalent to severely limiting the sovereignty of developing nations in regard to their natural resources—a limitation distinctly beneficial to industrial nations and their multinational corporations.

Considerable progress was achieved at the third meeting of the Group of 40 but it concluded without agreement on many basic issues because the industrial nations balked at making concessions.

*   *   *

The fourth meeting of the Group of 40 took place at the Mexican Ministry of Foreign Affairs in Tlatelolco section of Mexico City between June 10 and 28, 1974. This was undoubtedly the most productive meeting of the group. Its goal was to prepare a definitive draft of the Charter of Economic Rights and Duties of States and to approve the report to be presented to the Trade and Development Board, the executive organ of the United Nations Conference on Trade and Development. The greater part of the draft drawn up at this meeting was subsequently approved by the United Nations General Assembly on December 12, 1974.

A consensus was obtained on fundamental principles such as the responsibility of each state to "promote the economic, social and cultural development of its people" as well as to "cooperate in facilitating more rational and equitable international economic relations and in encouraging structural changes in the context of a balanced world economy in harmony with the needs and interests of all countries, especially developing countries."

Another point on which agreement was reached became Article 10 of Chapter II of the charter. This article states that "All States are *juridically* equal and, as equal members of the international community, have the right to participate fully and effectively in the international decision-making process in the solution of world economic, financial and monetary problems . . ." [Emphasis added.]

The fact that decisions on vital international issues were

previously made almost exclusively by the great powers under-scored the importance of achieving agreement on the principle of juridical equality of nations: "Juridically, this Charter . . . repre-sents the end of an era in history when international law es-tablished universal rules without the participation of the im-poverished nations which, without having approved them, had to obey them."

The Tlatelolco meeting was also notable for unanimity by the Group of 40 on thirty-six paragraphs comprising 80% of the proposed charter's text. Nevertheless, some very important issues remained unresolved because the viewpoint of the nations of the Group of 77 and the developed countries remained highly di-vergent.

When no agreement was reached on the remaining issues, some delegates began to feel pessimistic and frustrated over the in-transigent position held by the United States and other industrial nations. This situation became so serious that the new secretary-General of UNCTAD, Dr. Germani Corea, declared on June 19: "It will be a great shame if no decision is made to approve the charter, which is a document of universal application to be en-joyed and exercised by all nations."

At this point an enormous effort was expended in search of a consensus. Some socialist nations, such as Rumania and China, quickly identified with the Group of 77. But other nations in-cluding the United States, Japan, and West Germany—gave no indication of willingness to yield on vital issues such as the sovereignty of nations over their economic natural resources, the activities of multinational corporations, the nationalization of corporations, and the treatment of foreign investment. The de-veloping nations, as well as China and Rumania, took the follow-ing position:

"Each State has full and permanent sovereignty over its wealth and national resources.

"Each State has the right to regulate and control foreign in-vestment in accordance with its laws and regulations and in conformity with its own development objectives and priorities . . . No State whose nationals invest in a foreign country shall demand preferential treatment for such investors."

The Third World position on multinational corporations was unequivocal: "Each State has the right to regulate and control, in conformity with its laws, rules and regulations, transnational corporations within its national jurisdiction and take measures to assure that such corporations comply fully with said laws."

A different view, including not only the rights of the host government but also the right of the multinational corporation to equality of treatment, was advanced by several members of the European Common Market: "Each State shall assure that transnational corporations are subject within its national jurisdiction to the same laws and fulfill the same obligations of any other legal person [i.e., including corporations, which are legally "persons."] All States should cooperate in good faith with regard to the application of their respective laws to transnational corporations."

The text suggested by the United States stated: "Each State shall treat transnational corporations impartially and in a non-discriminatory manner, and shall moreover observe applicable international obligations." Another proposal from the developed countries included a clause requiring a State nationalizing the assets of a transnational corporation to pay it "just compensation."

International obligations applicable to the proposition of nationalization were allusions to United Nations Resolution 1803, which stipulates that compensation must be just, prompt and effective. This stipulation prevents small nations from nationalizing multinational corporations which often operate worldwide on far greater budgets than the developing host nation itself.

To sum up, the position held by the industrial nations was that the great multinational corporations, many of them international monopolies, should be treated like sovereign states protected by an international code of law. Obviously such a position was unacceptable to the developing countries. The Third World nations held firm to the position that Dr. Echeverria expressed at UNCTAD

III—namely, that a compromise limiting the principle of sovereignty in favor of profit-seeking multinational corporations was unacceptable.

A related controversy between the industrial and developing nations stemmed from the declaration of full sovereignty and continuing rights to natural resources. The nations better able to exploit such resources were unwilling to submit to restrictions in the appropriation of resources not belonging to them. The developed countries insisted that all nations offer special guarantees to multinational corporations. Mexico and other countries viewed this as absurd, noting that their constitutions include provisions regulating foreign investments and forbidding monopolies. Such provision, moreover, was unacceptable to nations which have experienced the damaging effects of the uncontrolled actions of multinational corporations.

The Peruvian delegate, in opposing a draft proposal on multinational corporations made by West Germany on behalf of the European Economic Community, the United States, and Japan, declared that such a narrow viewpoint ran counter to the spirit of the United Nations' declarations and made no viable contribution to the solution of the situation experienced by developing nations regarding the regulation and control of multinational corporations.

Although much of the draft charter was completed and the Group of 40 had agreed to the Preamble, Chapters I and II, as well as sixteen articles in Chapter II, two issues remained unresolved and continued to cause friction—the right to nationalize foreign investments and the question of compensation. In other respects the agreement at Tlatelolco was highly gratifying. It emphasized the sovereign right of each state to choose its economic, political, social and cultural systems without interference as well as the duty of the more developed states to cooperate in helping less developed countries. Agreement was also reached on active participation of all nations in solving economic and financial problems, the need to strengthen and improve the operation of in-

ternational organizations, the utilization of scientific and technological advances, the need to expand and liberalize world trade,
endorsement of international cooperation to hasten the economic
and social growth of developing nations, the use and expansion
of generalized tariff preferences for developing nations, and the
expansion of trade between developing nations and the countries
of the socialist bloc, and among the developing nations themselves.

Agreement was also reached on the right of all states to participate in world trade involving transportation, tourism, etc. The
need to prevent economic relations from prejudicing the interest
of developing nations was stressed, and special attention was
drawn to the problems of the most underdeveloped countries.

Failure to agree on remaining articles of the draft charter
which dealt with methods of international trade mirrored the
existing conflict between the nations of the European economic
community and the socialist bloc. The Bulgarian representative
interpreted the spirit of Dr. Echeverria's proposal by observing
that the charter should not only address itself to the solution of
concrete problems but also to general improvement in the economic and trade relations between nations. In his opinion it was
essential that Chapter II contain provisions against trade discrimination based on differences in economic and social systems. He
also urged that most-favored-nation treatment be included as a
general rule of international trade.

Owing to the intransigence of some industrial nations, the
Tlatelolco meeting ended without achieving full agreement on all
the provisions of the charter. The chairman of the Group of 40
referred to this in his closing speech when he charged that the
struggle of small nations to achieve economic independence and
to consolidate their democratic institutions "was hindered by
obviously neocolonial interests . . . by people who refuse to
recognize changes in the world of today" and who sought "to
compromise the very essence of national sovereignty and the

self-determination of peoples—an essential precondition to all civilized coexistence."

The situation at the end of the fourth session of the Group of 40 meeting can be summed up as follows: the Third World nations which sought an unemasculated version of Dr. Echeverria's charter would have to seek direct approval by the United Nations General Assembly. At the end of the meeting, Dr. Echeverria stated flatly that "Mexico believes it is totally unacceptable to endow multinational corporations with rights which legitimately belong to independent and sovereign nations. The United States must understand that these corporations are and indeed must be subject to the domestic laws of the host nation."

The Group of 40 recommended that new consultations take place with a view to settling unresolved differences. These consultations took place during a special session of UNCTAD's Trade and Development Board. When the 29th session of the United Nations General Assembly convened, a single draft Charter of Economic Rights and Duties of States together with all pertinent amendments was submitted to the Second Commission of the Economic and Social Council. Despite the vicissitudes experienced throughout its preparation the draft finally presented to the United Nations General Assembly retained all the vigor of Dr. Echeverria's original proposal.

*　　*　　*

The General Assembly is the heart of the United Nations. All member states are represented in it, and each is entitled to one vote. The Assembly meets once a year in ordinary session. It organizes its work through two basic bodies: the Security Council and the Economic and Social Council. During the course of the Assembly's sessions, the most important international problems of the day are discussed and frequently solved.

The developing nations have considerable strength in the Assembly. By sheer numbers they constitute the majority of member states. Their activities deserve great credit for the UN's recognition of the right to development. Moreover, their support has virtually been the backbone of the Economic and Social Council (ECOSOC), the UN's five regional Economic Commissions, and organizations such as UNCTAD and the Commission on the Law of the Sea.

According to the provisions of Resolution 45 pertaining to the third United Nations Conference on Trade and Development and General Assembly Resolution 3037, the Charter of Economic Rights and Duties of States was to be ready for debate before the General Assembly at its 28th session in 1973. But the difficulties encountered by the Group of 40, largely stemming from antagonism between industrial and developing nations, led to a long and complex process of adjustment. The Assembly therefore decided to put off debate on the charter for another year.

In consequence, the charter was assigned to the Assembly's Second Committee and placed on the agenda for the sessions beginning in September, 1974. Towards the end of November of that year, Mexico—with the support of more than a hundred nations—presented to the Second Committee a draft resolution on the charter outlining the antecedents and considerations upon which it was based, and urged that it be promptly discussed and approved by the Assembly.

The Second Committee received several amendments to the Mexican draft resolution, the majority of which were approved by the representatives of the very nations which later would vote against the charter.

In the early days of December, 1974, after consulting with the representatives of various nations, Mexico presented in the name of its sponsors a number of revisions of its draft resolution. Almost simultaneously the French delegation introduced a new draft resolution on the same topic in its own name and in behalf of Belgium, Denmark, Ireland, Italy, Luxembourg, the Netherlands, the United Kingdom, and West Germany. This draft paid tribute to the great interest that the charter held for the entire international community, but it contended that such a document should reflect general agreement among all the nations involved.

Since there were still many controversial issues at stake, the French delegation requested that the working group persist in its efforts to achieve a consensus on the charter and suggested that this group's report be presented to the General Assembly at its extraordinary session on "International Economic Development and Cooperation" in September, 1975. In essence, this tactic reflected, in a none too subtle fashion, basic disagreement by the industrial nations with the spirit and content of the charter. The primary purpose of delaying the charter was to assure continuation of the status quo—i.e., continuation of the existing economic relations subject to the law of the strongest nations. There was nothing strange in this. The issues which the industrial nations sought to alter in the charter—nationalization, multinational corporations, foreign investments, and the right of producing nations to act jointly—were precisely the most important questions the nations of the Third World desired to resolve. After two and a half years of discussion it appeared unlikely that a consensus would ever be reached.

The draft resolution presented by France was rejected by a vote of 81 against, 20 in favor and 15 abstentions. The amendments proposed by France were also scuttled.

The revised draft resolution sponsored by Mexico was then put to a committee vote, paragraph by paragraph and article by article. When this was done, the charter was voted on as a whole and approved by 115 votes in favor, with six against and ten abstentions. Accordingly the Second Committee recommended approval of the charter by the General Assembly.

In this way, 32 months after the original proposal was first offered by Dr. Echeverria, the charter was adopted by the United Nations on December 12, 1974, as a set of principles and rules for the regulation of the economic relations between states and establishment of a new world order based on international respect and cooperation.

In the General Assembly, there were 120 nations in favor of the charter with ten abstaining and six against. Of the other two members of the United Nations, South Africa did not have the right to vote, and the representative of the Falkland Islands was absent.

The nations which voted in favor of the adoption of the Charter of Economic Rights and Duties of States were:

Afghanistan	Greece	Pakistan
Albania	Guatemala	Panama
Algeria	Guinea	Peru
Argentina	Guinea-Bissau	Paraguay
Australia	Guyana	Philippines
Bahamas	Haiti	Poland
Bahrein	Honduras	Portugal
Bangladesh	Hungary	Qatar
Barbados	Iceland	Rumania
Bhutan	India	Rwanda
Bolivia	Indonesia	Saudi Arabia
Botswana	Iran	Senegal
Brazil	Iraq	Sierra Leone
Bulgaria	Ivory Coast	Singapore
Burma	Jamaica	Somalia
Burundi	Jordan	Sri Lanka
Byelorussian SSR	Kenya	Sudan
Cameroon	Khmer Rep.	Swaziland
Central African Rep.	Kuwait	Sweden
Chad	Laos	Syria
Chile	Lebanon	Tanzania
China	Lesotho	Thailand
Colombia	Liberia	Togo
Congo	Libya	Trinidad and Tobago
Costa Rica	Madagascar	Tunisia
Cuba	Malawi	Turkey
Cyprus	Malaysia	Uganda
Czechoslovakia	Maldive Islands	Ukranian SSR
Dahomey	Mali	USSR
Dominican Rep.	Malta	United Arab
Ecuador	Mauritania	Emirates
Ecuatorial Guinea	Mauritius	Upper Volta
Egypt	Mexico	Uruguay
El Salvador	Mongolia	Venezuela
Ethiopia	Morocco	Yemen
Fiji	Nepal	Yemen (PDRY)
Finland	New Zealand	Yugoslavia
Gabon	Nicaragua	Zaire
Gambia	Niger	Zambia
German Dem. Rep.	Nigeria	
Ghana	Oman	

The six nations that voted against the charter were the United States and five members of the European Economic Community—

Belgium, Denmark, the Federal Republic of Germany, Luxembourg, and the United Kingdom. The ten abstention votes were cast by Austria, Canada, France, Ireland, Israel, Italy, Japan, the Netherlands, Norway, and Spain.

A United Nations resolution such as the charter is juridically highly significant in view of the fact that the overwhelming majority which approved it represent eighty percent of the world population. Therefore, even though the General Assembly's resolutions do not entail coercive action, the effect of world public opinion exerts a powerful moral influence. Moreover, the possibility still exists that even countries which abstained or voted against the charter may soon be won over to the advantages it offers the world.

8: The Significance
of a Far-Reaching Charter

The final text of the Charter of Economic Rights and Duties of States as approved by the United Nations General Assembly is a cogently written document.

Its main objective is to overcome the injustice prevailing in economic relations between nations and eliminate the dependence of Third World countries on industrial nations. Accordingly it lays down a set of fundamental principles and rules for the regulation of economic relations that have for too long been responsible for irrational and unfair practices. These principles and rules are based on the equal sovereignty of nations seeking cooperatively to build a new world order.

There are five main sources from which the charter is derived. First are the principles established by international law, especially with regard to the peaceful settlement of disputes, the equal sovereignty of states, and non-intervention. The second source is the set of principles and procedures adopted at recent international conferences particularly at the sessions of the United Nations Conferences on Trade and Development. The abolition of protective tariffs, the common use of world resources, and non-reciprocal preferential treatment are examples of such principles.

The charter's third important source stems from ideological principles of the Mexican Revolution embodied in the provisions of the Mexican Constitution of 1917, particularly concerning social justice. The fourth of the charter's origins derives from the ideas and ethics of Dr. Echeverria, the humanist President of Mexico; without his inspiration and drive the charter would not be what it is. Finally the fifth source arises from hopes and aspirations of the nations of the Third World for progress, justice and peace.

The ideas of the charter are many but some rise above the others—for example, the appeal for international cooperation and the protection of national sovereignty over resources traditionally exploited by imperialist powers. Moreover, the charter embodies principles that contribute to the resolution of pressing international problems such as worldwide inflation, the deterioration of the environment, etc. These problems involve rich and poor nations alike; their repercussions affect the whole of humanity.

The Preamble and Chapter I of the Charter of Economic Rights and Duties of States set forth the considerations, aims, and fundamental principles on which the economic relations between nations should rest. One of the most important of these objectives is the establishment of an equitable international economic order. The Preamble as a whole is not limited to the economic sphere; it applies to matters as diverse as the protection and improvement of the environment, scientific and technological cooperation, the right of nations to control their natural resources, and the recognition of political pluralism in international affairs, in essence, the charter aspires to the transformation of an international society based exclusively on power into one based on genuine world cooperation.

The principles of the new economic order formulated in Chapter I reassert traditional principles of international law and it extends them beyond the political sphere into the realm of social justice. The charter thus pertains to matters such as sovereignty, the territorial integrity and independence of states, non-aggression, peaceful coexistence, reparations for past injustices imposed by force, international cooperation for development, the right of free passage to and from the sea by landlocked nations, and repudiation of the policy of apartheid and other forms of colonialism.

Chapter II, the principal juridical portion of the charter, spells out in 28 articles the economic rights and duties of states. The very first article rejects ideological intolerance and emphasizes the right of each state to choose its own destiny without interference, coercion or threat of any kind. This constitutes the basis for the charter's principle of national sovereignty. The latter is a clear projection of Article 39 of the Mexican Constitution: "National sovereignty essentially and originally stems from the will of the people. Public power derives from the people and is established for their benefit. The people always have the inalienable right to change or alter their type of government."

Sovereignty as an essential attribute of the people is one of the chief elements of national assertion with respect to other countries. A necessary complement of this principle is sovereign equality— i.e., the sovereignty of each nation over its natural resources and the self-determination of its people as well as explicit recognition that the sovereignty of all nations, large and small, has equal standing before the international community.

Article 2, which bolsters the right of national ownership of natural resources, was the subject of much debate during the charter's preparation and it became one of the reasons why six industrial countries voted against the charter in the United Nations General Assembly. This principle has been recognized by Mexican law since 1917, when Article 27 became part of that nation's Constitution. This article states: "The ownership of land and sea within the limits of the national patrimony belongs originally to the Nation . . ."

Linked with sovereignty over natural resources is the problem of foreign investment which developing nations view with mixed feelings of fear and hope. The reason for this duality is that foreign investment, when it conforms to national objectives, is an invaluable source of the supplementary capital and technology that poor nations need but it becomes a serious handicap when it is used by highly industrial nations as a pretext for diplomatic pressures and military intervention.

Multinational corporations have been instrumental in increasing the economic dependence of developing nations on industrial nations by limiting their ability to exercise sovereignty and by blocking their social and economic objectives. One of the most damaging

results has been the transformation of developing nations into highly specialized producers of one or two crops, which in turn has
deepened economic dependence on multinational corporations. This
inevitably makes developing countries easy prey to nations that
buy large quantities of raw materials, the price of which varies in
the international market in response to the interests of multinational corporations or industrial nations.

But the major drawback in regard to multinational corporations
has been their interference in the domestic affairs of Third World
nations. In fact, many of these enormous corporations have acquired the characteristics of national governments. The decisions
they make—whether to invest, change prices, reduce or expand
production, export, automate a plant or introduce new technologies—have tremendous impact on the economic, social, and political systems of the host nations. Because they operate in several
countries simultaneously, these corporations are practically in a
position to determine the conditions under which they carry on
their business, particularly in regard to labor costs, tariffs, rates
of interest, etc.

The political power exerted by multinational corporations becomes exceedingly onerous when they evade the control and jurisdiction of the nations in which they operate. Nations victimized by
the activities of these corporations find their meddling in domestic
affairs quite intolerable. Therefore, subordination of multinational corporations to national laws is a *sine qua non* of any policy
of independent economic and social development. Mexico, it
should be noted, was one of the first countries to assert its sovereignty over its natural resources and take a firm stand against
multinational corporations.

Another principle laid down in the charter is the right of nations producing primary comodities to associate in defense of
common interests—a right closely linked to the principles of international equality, sovereignty and self-determination. The recent
implementation of this right by some small countries has elicited
from the large industrial nations a medley of belligerent declara-

tions and hostile measures such as the Foreign Trade Law enacted by the U.S. Congress several years ago despite the fact that the right of association set forth in the charter's fifth article corresponds to present international practice and provides third world nations with an effective tool against the machinations of industrial countries.

The right of association endorsed by the charter is especially important because a weak nation standing alone can do little or nothing to defend itself against the economic aggression of far stronger nations and corporations but the situation can be radically altered if weak countries band together. Ironically, the nations which most vociferously opposed inclusion of Article 5 in the charter are themselves members of a bloc of nations known as the European Economic Community (Common Market).

Although industrial nations have exercised the right of association for many years, developing nations that have sought to do the same have been frustrated by pressures from multinational corporations and/or industrial nations. When, for example, several Central American nations tried to obtain a better price for their banana exports, they encountered strong resistance.

Another aspect of the clear right of association by commodity producing nations must be mentioned. It is the asserted but non-existent right that some nations exercise in carrying out punitive measures against developing nations which insist they are entitled to conduct their affairs with the full benefit of the self-determination and non-intervention principles sanctioned by present international law. The application of discriminatory economic measures against nations which exercise their right of association constitutes flagrant intervention. That is why the foreign trade laws of the U. S. have been so vehemently criticized.

The charter's explicit recognition of ideas embodying the political pluralism and juridical equality of nations is highly important. As the bipolar system of international relations has deteriorated, a political and ideological pluralism has emerged. Today realistic trade policy cannot be based on discrimination against nations with different economic, social or political systems. Discriminatory practices are equivalent to violation of national sovereignty, self-determination and non-intervention.

The juridical equality of states established by Article 10 of the charter is another principle derived from the recognition of national sovereignty and international equity. Juridical equality has been traditionally understood to mean that all states have the same rights and obligations. Uniform treatment of unequal entities, however, is unjust. One cannot expect all nations to incur the same obligations if they do not enjoy the same benefits. In the realm of international law, the inequality of states should not give rise to unequal treatment but to efforts to equalize the imbalance by giving greater advantages to those who find themselves in disadvantaged positions. This means that political and juridical equality must be complemented with a system of nonreciprocal preferences conducive to economic equality.

In terms of international social justice, particularly as it applies to the principle of distributive justice, juridical and political equality imply active participation in the decisions of the international community under equal circumstances. They also imply the obligation of industrial nations to aid developing nations in raising the standard of living of their people. One of the methods for accomplishing this is to extend economic trade advantages in proportion to the states' level of development.

The charter rejects the traditional concept of juridical equality and bases its view on the international principle of social justice. The importance of the social justice concept in helping to break the vicious circle of poverty and dependence of developing nations cannot be overestimated. It may not be easy to implement but the outlook for the Third World nations is very promising.

The Charter of Economic Rights and Duties of States is a pacifist document in that Article 15 deals with disarmament as an essential factor in a new international order based on security and cooperation instead of fear and the destructive capacity of nuclear weapons. Mindful that the economy of industrial nations is partially dependent on the production of weapons, the charter advocates the application of financial, human and scientific resources to health, education, and other means of improving the lot of mankind, particularly among two-thirds of the world's people inhabiting the developing nations. In short, the chapter opts for the love of life rather than for the death wish of the world's merchants of destruction.

War continues to be waged with conventional weapons because the concept of "nuclear parity" and the catastrophic potential of nuclear weapons have rendered them inefficacious. Moreover, since atomic weapons have also ceased to be useful as a deterrent, maintaining an economy on a war footing is historically absurd, economically mistaken, and politically shortsighted.

*   *   *

It is generally realized that development and growth are quite different, although some experts have strained their definitions in order to treat them as synonymous. Growth is a process by which a quantitative accumulation of goods and services is obtained; development, on the other hand, is a process by which a structural change takes place so that these same goods and services are made available to the people. Whereas growth means an increase in the gross national product, development means the improvement of the standard of living. The first is a quantitative concept; the second is qualitative, and apart from its purely economic connotations, has social, political, and cultural implications.

The concern for economic, social, and cultural development experienced by all nations, especially those of the Third World, is clearly enunciated in Articles 6, 7, 8, and 9 of the charter. Making each state responsible for its own development implies that resources must be mobilized in accordance with the objectives a state has chosen in the exercise of its full sovereignty. The charter establishes that responsibility be shared by the industrial nations and the international community in promoting the development of Third World nations.

The political, social, and cultural development of a people is closely linked to its level of economic development. The latter in turn is necessarily dependent on political, social, and cultural policies. Therefore, given the extraordinary interdependence which exists among the economies of all nations, the repercussions of economic measures adopted by one country are intensely felt by other countries—particularly when their level of development is lower. This is why regulation of international economic relations is a fundamental requirement of the charter.

If international economic equity is to be achieved, the developing nations must play a more active role in the decision-making process of the international community. It is clearly unacceptable for a small number of nations to make decisions affecting all nations or that any nation should be expected to comply with arrangements to which it is not a party. The charter's tenth and twelfth articles confirm the right of all nations, including the smallest and weakest, to join in international decision-making processes.

While it is true that developing nations face serious problems with respect to their dependence in trade and financial matters, their dependence in regard to technology is even more acute. The lack of an indigenous technology compels such nations to rely on the technology of industrial nations. But acquiring and adapting outside technology is somewhat complicated. The shortage of labor in highly industrialized nations has led them to devise technologies requiring a high level of investment and reduced manpower. The conditions in developing nations are exactly the opposite; they have an abundance of manpower and a shortage of capital.

As we now know all too well, much of the technology devised by industrial nations has been exceedingly noxious to the environment. Recently, having become uneasy about their responsibility for the pollution of the atmosphere and the seas, some industrial nations have created costly antipollutant technologies which are far beyond the means of developing nations. Moreover, a major portion of the technology exported by industrial nations, particularly by their powerful multinational corporations, is regarded as both wasteful and noxious in its own country of origin.

This explains why technological dependence is a primary concern of the charter. Article 13 lays down the conditions under which the conveyance of technology from industrial nations to developing nations should take place; the right of the latter to benefit by scientific and technical advances is considered part of mankind's patrimony.

In discussing the problems and consequences arising from the transfer of technology, Dr. Echeverria called attention to his country's policy: "Mexico increasingly needs equipment and technology. To obtain them without impairing its independence and monetary stability, it is necessary that the acquisition of knowledge and capital goods be free of all constraints and that we be really able to choose the techniques and procedures which best apply to our economic conditions."

True to the charter's humanistic and democratic purposes, Article 16 emphatically condemns discrimination based on the color of skin and all other forms of racial oppression. The policy of "apartheid" means, of course, "separate development". Since the majority of the population of South Africa is black, "apartheid" is patently designed to maintain the predominance of the white minority. This policy has been justified on the ground that its objective is to provide the same opportunities to all races, but the fact remains that it is a domestic type of colonialism entailing the domination of one sector of the population by another.

The chief aim of the so-called "general system of preferences", as incorporated in Article 19, is to by-pass tariff barriers and open the markets of industrial nations to the manufactured and semi-manufactured products of developing nations. Although the subsidiaries of some multinational corporations have profited by this system, the effect on the developing nations, by and large, has been beneficial. In order to improve this process, the charter endorses the principle of "general, nonreciprocal, nondiscriminatory preferential treatment" as a means of extending the advantages of the system to all developing nations and discouraging industrial nations from using preferences to exert pressure on smaller nations. Additionally, the nonreciprocal feature is a necessary corollary of the charter's principles of economic justice.

Cooperation as the foundation for a new international economic order is the obvious concern of Articles 20 and 27. As is implicit in these articles, the relations between states must be regulated by a code of rules delineating what is permissable without forgetting that the developing nations are the weakest link in the chain. Accordingly, the charter warns that all measures prejudicial to the interests of developing nations must be avoided and calls upon the industrial nations to help Third World nations through genuine, not pro forma, cooperation.

Article 28 deals with the unequal price relationship between primary commodities and manufactured products. Industrial nations sell their goods at a higher price than developing nations sell their primary commodities. This has contributed substantially to the economic dependence, loss of capital, and foreign indebtedness of Third World nations. Article 28 requires all states to cooperate for the purpose of ensuring that the ratio between the prices developing nations pay for their imports and receive for their exports is just and stable. It is, indeed, more desirable for developing nations to obtain just and stable prices for the primary commodities they export than an increase in the financial aid they receive from industrial nations and international organizations. Article 28 satisfies one of the most important claims of Third World nations.

Articles 29 and 30 spell out the common responsibilities of nations to the international community. Article 29 declares that the seabed and the oceanic depths outside national jurisdictions belong to all mankind. The importance of this is that the search for food is expected to intensify exploitation of the resources of the seas. The charter stipulates that the benefits derived from maritime resources should be shared equitably among the nations and not enjoyed exclusively by technologically advanced states.

Conservation and improvement of the environment are the concern of Article 30. The problems stemming from pollution pose one of the gravest threats to our planet. In manipulating nature for his comfort, man has broken the ecological balance and limited nature's capacity for recycling and reabsorbing the elements. Although industrial man is chiefly to blame for polluting and destroying the ecological balance, the preservation of the environment which makes human life possible is the responsibility of all nations. Mindful of the charter's principle of sovereignty, Article 30 also recognizes that each state is free to determine its own environmental policies, but it calls upon all states to join in the formulation of international regulations in this field.

Article 31 deals with the obligation of all states to "contribute to the balanced expansion of the world economy" in the light of its profoundly interdependent characteristics.

Article 32 expressly forbids the use of economic, political and other measures as methods of coercion against a state. This practice is all too common and imposes serious limitations on the exercise of national sovereignty.

Article 33 provides guidance as to how the charter's provisions should be interpreted, emphasizing that they should not "be construed as impairing or derogating from the provisions of the Charter of the United Nations or actions taken in pursuance thereof." The second paragraph of this article emphasizes that none of the provisions of the Charter of Economic Rights and Duties of States should be viewed as separate from the others. Each must be interpreted in relation to the remainder of the charter.

Article 34, the charter's last provision, requires the United Nations General Assembly to consider revision of the charter every five years in view of new conditions necessitating "improvements and additions."

The charter is the only available option that will help surmount the postwar world economic crisis and establish a new world order based on equitable economic relations between nations.

The world of the future will be less unjust and less ridden with anxiety, more secure and better able to care for its own if we respect the principles of the charter.

TEXT OF THE CHARTER OF

ECONOMIC RIGHTS AND DUTIES OF STATES

PREAMBLE

The General Assembly,

Reaffirming the fundamental purposes of the United Nations, in particular, the maintenance of international peace and security, the development of friendly relations among nations and the achievement of international co-operation in solving international problems in the economic and social fields,

Affirming the need for strengthening international co-operation in these fields,

Reaffirming further the need for strengthening international co-operation for development,

Declaring that it is a fundamental purpose of this Charter to promote the establishment of the new international economic order, based on equity, sovereign equality, interdependence, common interest and co-operation among all States, irrespective of their economic and social systems,

Desirous of contributing to the creation of conditions for:

(a) The attainment of wider prosperity among all countries and of higher standards of living for all peoples,

(b The promotion by the entire international community of economic and social progress of all countries, especially developing countries,

(c The encouragement of co-operation, on the basis of mutual advantage and equitable benefits for all peace-loving States which are willing to carry out the provisions of this Charter, in the economic, trade, scientific and technical fields, regardless of political, economic or social systems,

(d) The overcoming of main obstacles in the way of the economic development of the developing countries,

(e) The acceleration of the economic growth of developing countries with a view to bridging the economic gap between developing and developed countries,

(f) The protection, preservation and enhancement of the environment,

Mindful of the need to establish and maintain a just and equitable economic and social order through:

(a) The achievement of more rational and equitable international economic relations and the encouragement of structural changes in the world economy.

(b) The creation of conditions which permit the further expansion of trade and intensification of economic co-operation among all nations,

(c) The strengthening of the economic independence of developing countries,

(d) The establishment and promotion of international economic relations, taking into account the agreed differences in development of the developing countries and their specific needs,

Determined to promote collective economic security for development, in particular of the developing countries, with strict respect for the sovereign equality of each State and through the co-operation of the entire international community,

Considering that genuine co-operation among States, based on joint consideration of and concerted action regarding international economic problems, is essential for fulfilling the international community's common desire to achieve a just and rational development of all parts of the world,

Stressing the importance of ensuring appropriate conditions for the conduct of normal economic relations among all States, irrespective of differences in social and economic systems, and for the full respect for the rights of all peoples, as well as the strengthening of instruments of international economic co-operation as means for the consolidation of peace for the benefit of all,

Convinced of the need to develop a system of international economic relations on the basis of sovereign equality, mutual and equitable benefit and the close interrelationship of the interests of all States,

Reiterating that the responsibility for the development of every country rests primarily upon itself by that concomitant and effective international co-operation is an essential factor for the full achievement of its own development goals,

Firmly convinced of the urgent need to evolve a substantially improved system of international economic relations,

Solemnly adopts the present Charter of Economic Rights and Duties of States.

Chapter I

Fundamentals of International Economic Relations

Economic as well as political and other relations among States shall be governed, *inter alia,* by the following principles:

(a) Sovereignty, territorial integrity and political independence of States;

(b) Sovereign equality of all States;

(c) Non-aggression;

(d) Non-intervention;

(e) Mutual and equitable benefit;

(f) Peaceful coexistence;

(g) Equal rights and self-determination of peoples;

(h) Peaceful settlement of disputes;

(i) Remedying of injustices which have been brought about by force and which deprive a nation of the natural means necessary for its normal development;

(j) Fulfilment in good faith of international obligations;

(k) Respect for human rights and fundamental freedoms;

(l) No attempt to seek hegemony and spheres of influence;

(m) Promotion of international social justice;

(n) International co-operation for development;

(o) Free access to and from the sea by land-locked countries within the framework of the above principles.

Chapter II

Economic Rights and Duties of States

Article 1

Every State has the sovereign and inalienable right to choose its economic system as well as its political, social and cultural systems in accordance with the will of its people without outside interference, coercion or threat in any form whatsoever.

Article 2

1. Every State has and shall freely exercise full permanent sovereignty,

including possession, use and disposal, over all its wealth, natural resources and economic activities.

2. Each State has the right:

(a) To regulate and exercise authority over foreign investment within its national jurisdiction in accordance with its laws and regulations and in conformity with its national objectives and priorities. No State shall be compelled to grant preferential treatment to foreign investment:

(b) To regulate and supervise the activities of transnational corporations within its national jurisdiction and take measures to ensure that such activities comply with its laws, rules and regulations and conform with its economic and social policies. Transnational corporations shall not intervene in the internal affairs of a host State. Every State should, with full regard for its sovereign rights, co-operate with other States in the exercise of the right set forth in this subparagraph;

(c) To nationalize, expropriate or transfer ownership of foreign property, in which case appropriate compensation would be paid by the State adopting such measures, taking into account its relevant laws and regulations and all circumstances that the State considers pertinent. In any case where the question of compensation gives rise to a controversy, it shall be settled under the domestic law of the nationalizing State and by its tribunals, unless it is freely and mutually agreed by all States concerned that other peaceful means be sought on the basis of the sovereign equality of States and in accordance with the principle of free choice of means.

Article 3

In the exploitation of natural resources shared by two or more countries, each State must co-operate on the basis of a system of information and prior consultations in order to achieve optimum use of such resources without causing damage to the legitimate interest of others.

Article 4

Every State has the right to engage in international trade and other forms of economic co-operation irrespective of any differences in political, economic and social systems. No State shall be subjected to discrimination of any kind based solely on such differences. In the pursuit of international trade and other forms of economic co-operations, every State is free to choose the forms of organization of its foreign economic relations and to enter into bilateral and multilateral arrangements consistent with its international obligations and with the needs of international economic co-operation.

Article 5

All States have the right to associate in organizations of primary commodity producers in order to develop their national economies to achieve stable financing for their development, and in pursuance of their aims, to assist in the promotion of sustained growth of the world economy, in particular accelerating the development of developing countries. Correspondingly all States have the duty to respect that right by refraining from applying economic and political measures that would limit it.

Article 6

It is the duty of States to contribute to the development of international trade of goods, particularly by means of arrangements and by the conclusion of long-term multilateral commodity agreements, where appropriate, and taking into account the interests of producers and consumers. All States share the responsibility to promote the regular flow and access of all commercial goods traded at stable, remunerative and equitable prices, thus contributing to the equitable development of the world economy, taking into account, in particular, the interests of developing countries.

Article 7

Every State has the primary responsibility to promote the economic, social and cultural development of its people. To this end, each State has the right and the responsibility to choose its means and goals of development, fully to mobilize and use its resources, to implement progressive economic and social reforms and to ensure the full participation of its people in the process and benefits of development. All States have the duty, individually and collectively, to co-operate in order to eliminate obstacles that hinder such mobilization and use.

Article 8

States should co-operate in facilitating more rational and equitable international economic relations and in encouraging structural changes in the context of a balanced world economy in harmony with the needs and interests of all countries, especially developing countries, and should take appropriate measures to this end.

Article 9

All States have the responsibility to co-operate in the economic, social, cultural, scientific and technological fields for the promotion of economic and social progress throughout the world, especially that of the developing countries.

Article 10

All States are juridically equal and, as equal members of the international community, have the right to participate fully and effectively in the international decision-making process in the solution of world economic, financial and monetary problems, *inter alia*, through the appropriate international organizations in accordance with their existing and evolving rules, and to share equitably in the benefits resulting therefrom.

Article 11

All States should co-operate to strengthen and continuously improve the efficiency of international organizations in implementing measures to stimulate the general economic progress of all countries, particularly of developing countries, and therefore should co-operate to adapt them, when appropriate, to the changing needs of international economic co-operation.

Article 12

1. States have the right, in agreement with the parties concerned, to participate in subregional, regional and interregional co-operation in the pursuit of their economic and social development. All States engaged in such co-operation have the duty to ensure that the policies of those groupings to which they belong correspond to the provisions of the Charter and are outward-looking, consistent with their international obligations and with the needs of international economic co-operation and have full regard for the legitimate interests of third countries, especially developing countries.

2. In the case of groupings to which the States concerned have transferred or may transfer certain competences as regards matters that come within the scope of the present Charter, its provisions shall also apply to those groupings, in regard to such matters, consistent with the responsibilities of such States as members of such groupings. Those States shall co-operate in the observance by the groupings of the provisions of this Charter.

Article 13

1. Every State has the right to benefit from the advances and developments in science and technology for the acceleration of its economic and social development.

2. All States should promote international scientific and technological

co-operation and the transfer of technology, with proper regard for all legitimate interests including, *inter alia,* the rights and duties of holders, suppliers and recipients of technology. In particular, all States should facilitate the access of developing countries to the achievements of modern science and technology, the transfer of technology and the creation of indigenous technology for the benefit of the developing countries in forms and in accordance with procedures which are suited to their economies and their needs.

3. Accordingly, developed countries should co-operate with the developing countries in the establishment, strengthening and development of their scientific and technological activities so as to help to expand and transform the economies of developing countries.

4. All States should co-operate in exploring with a view to evolving further internationally accepted guidelines or regulations for the transfer of technology, taking fully into account the interests of developing countries.

Article 14

Every State has the duty to co-operate in promoting a steady and increasing expansion and liberalization of world trade and an improvement in the welfare and living standards of all peoples in particular those of developing countries. Accordingly, all States should co-operate, *inter alia,* towards the progressive dismantling of obstacles to trade and the improvement of the international framework for the conduct of world trade and to these ends, co-ordinated efforts shall be made to solve in an equitable way the trade problems of all countries, taking into account the specific trade problems of the developing countries. In this connection, States shall take measures aimed at securing additional benefits for the international trade of developing countries so as to achieve a substantial increase in their foreign exchange earnings, the diversification of their exports, the acceleration of the rate of growth of their trade, taking into account their development needs, an improvement in the possibilities for these countries to participate in the expansion of world trade and a balance more favourable to developing countries in the sharing of the advantages resulting from this expansion, through, in the largest possible measure, substantial improvement in the conditions of access for the products of interest to the developing countries and, wherever appropriate, measures designed to attain stable, equitable and remunerative prices for primary products.

Article 15

All States have the duty to promote the achievement of general and complete disarmament under effective international control and to utilize the resources freed by effective disarmament measures for the economic and social development of countries, allocating a substantial portion of such resources as additional means for the development needs of developing countries.

Article 16

1. It is the right and duty of all States, individually and collectively, to eliminate colonialism, *apartheid,* racial discrimination, neo-colonialism and all forms of foreign aggression, occupation and domination, and the economic and social consequences thereof, as a prerequisite for development. States which practice such coercive policies are economically responsible to the countries, territories and peoples affected for the restitution and full compensation for the exploitation and depletion of, and damages to, the natural and all other resources of those countries, territories and peoples. It is the duty of all States to extend assistance to them.

2. No State has the right to promote or encourage investments that may constitute an obstacle to the liberation of a territory occupied by force.

Article 17

International co-operation for development is the shared goal and common duty of all States. Every State should co-operate with the efforts of developing countries to accelerate their economic and social development by providing favorable external conditions and by extending active assistance to them, consistent with their development needs and objectives, with strict respect for the sovereign equality of States and free of any conditions derogating from their sovereignty.

Article 18

Developed countries should extend, improve and enlarge the system of generalized non-reciprocal and non-discriminatory tariff preferences to the developing countries consistent with the relevant agreed conclusions and relevant decisions as adopted on this subject, in the framework of the competent international organizations. Developed countries should also give serious consideration to the adoption of other differential measures, in areas where this is feasible and appropriate and in ways which will provide special and more favorable treatment, in order to meet the trade and development needs of the developing countries. In the conduct of international economic relations the developed countries should endeavor to avoid measures having a negative effect on the development of the national economies of the developing countries, as promoted by generalized tariff preferences and other generally agreed differential measures in their favor.

Article 19

With a view to accelerating the economic growth of developing countries and bridging the economic gap between developed and developing countries, developed countries should grant generalized preferential, non-reciprocal and non-discriminatory treatment to developing countries in those fields of international economic co-operation where it may be feasible.

Article 20

Developing countries should, in their efforts to increase their over-all trade, give due attention to the possibility of expanding their trade with socialist countries, by granting to these countries conditions for trade not inferior to those granted normally to the developed market economy countries.

Article 21

Developing countries should endeavour to promote the expansion of their mutual trade and to this end may, in accordance with the existing and evolving provisions and procedures of international agreements where applicable, grant trade preferences to other developing countries without being obliged to extend such preferences to developed countries, provided these arrangements do not constitute an impediment to general trade liberalization and expansion.

Article 22

1. All States should respond to the generally recognized or mutually agreed development needs and objectives of developing countries by promoting increased net flows of real resources to the developing countries from all sources, taking into account any obligations and commitments undertaken by the States concerned, in order to reinforce the efforts of developing countries to accelerate their economic and social development.

2. In this context, consistent with the aims and objectives mentioned above and taking into account any obligations and commitments undertaken in this regard, it should be their endeavour to increase the net

amount of financial flows from official sources to developing countries and to improve the terms and conditions thereof.

3. The flow of development assistance resources should include economic and technical assistance.

Article 23

To enhance the effective mobilization of their own resources, the developing countries should strengthen their economic co-operation and expand their mutual trade so as to accelerate their economic and social development. All countries, especially developed countries, individually as well as through the competent international organizations of which they are members, should provide appropriate and effective support and co-operation.

Article 24

All States have the duty to conduct their mutual economic relations in a manner which takes into account the interests of other countries. In particular, all States should avoid prejudicing the interests of developing countries.

Article 25

In furtherance of world economic development, the international community, especially its developed members, shall pay special attention to the particular needs and problems of the least developed among the developing countries, of land-locked developing countries and also island developing countries, with a view to helping them to overcome their particular difficulties and thus contribute to their economic and social development.

Article 26

All States have the duty to coexist in tolerance and live together in peace, irrespective of differences in political, economic, social and cultural systems and to facilitate trade between States having different economic and social systems. International trade should be conducted without prejudice to generalized non-discriminatory and non-reciprocal preferences in favor of developing countries, on the basis of mutual advantage, equitable benefits and the exchange of most-favoured-nation treatment.

Article 27

1. Every State has the right to enjoy fully the benefits of world invisible trade and to engage in the expansion of such trade.

2. World invisible trade, based on efficiency and mutual and equitable benefit, furthering the expansion of the world economy, is the common goal of all States. The role of developing countries in world invisible trade should be enhanced and strengthened consistent with the above objectives, particular attention being paid to the special needs of developing countries.

3. All States should co-operate with developing countries in their endeavors to increase their capacity to earn foreign exchange from invisible transactions, in accordance with the potential and needs of each developing country and consistent with the objectives mentioned above.

Article 28

All States have the duty to co-operate in achieving adjustments in the prices of exports of developing countries in relation to prices of their imports so as to promote just and equitable terms of trade for them, in a manner which is remunerative for producers and equitable for producers and consumers.

Chapter III

Common Responsibilities Towards the International Community

Article 29

The sea-bed and ocean floor and the subsoil thereof, beyond the limits of national jurisdiction, as well as the resources of the area, are the common heritage of mankind. On the basis of the principles adopted by the General Assembly in resolution 2749 (XXV) of December 1970, all States shall ensure that the exploration of the area and exploitation of its resources are carried out exclusively for peaceful purposes and that the benefits derived therefrom are shared equitably by all States, taking into account the particular interests and needs of developing countries: an international regime applying to the area and its resources and including appropriate international machinery to give effect to its provisions shall be established by an international treaty of a universal character, generally agreed upon.

Article 30

The protection, preservation and the enhancement of the environment for the present and future generations is the responsibility of all States. All States shall endeavour to establish their own environmental and developmental policies in conformity with such responsibility. The environmental policies of all States should enhance and not adversely affect the present and future development potential of developing countries. All States have the responsibility to ensure that activities within their jurisdiction or control do not cause damage to the environment of other States or areas beyond the limits of national jurisdiction. All States should co-operate in evolving international norms and regulations in the field of the environment.

CHAPTER IV

FINAL PROVISIONS

Article 31

All States have the duty to contribute to the balanced expansion of the world economy, taking duly into account the close interrelationship between the well-being of the developed countries and the growth and development of the developing countries, and the fact that the prosperity of the international community as a whole depends upon the prosperity of its constituent parts.

Article 32

No State may use or encourage the use of economic, political or any other type of measures to coerce another State in order to obtain from it the subordination of the exercise of its sovereign rights.

Article 33

1. Nothing in the present Charter shall be construed as impairing or derogating from the provisions of the Charter of the United Nations or actions taken in pursuance thereof.

2. In their interpretation and application, the provisions of the present Charter are interrelated and each provision should be construed in the context of the other provisions.

Article 34

An item on the Charter of Economic Rights and Duties of States shall be inscribed in the agenda of the General Assembly at its thirtieth session, and thereafter on the agenda of every fifth session. In this way a systematic and comprehensive consideration of the implementation of the Charter, covering both progress achieved and any improvements and additions which might become necessary, would be carried out and appropriate measures recommended. Such consideration should take into account the evolution of all the economic, social, legal and other factors related to the principles upon which the present Charter is based and on its purpose.

APPENDIX B

TOWARD INTERNATIONAL DEMOCRACY

*Text of a speech by Dr. Luis Echeverria, President of Mexico,
on October 5, 1971, before the United Nations General Assembly*

Mr. President, on behalf of the people and Government of Mexico, I wish to convey to you our warmest congratulations on your well-deserved election, which ensures the impartiality and efficiency necessary to dispose properly of the items to be considered at this session.

Mexico's faith in our Organization remains unshaken, despite the setbacks to our Organization, since its continues to contribute in an even greater measure than is usually acknowledged to the development of the international community and because it fosters permanent dialogue among the nations of the world on a footing of legal equality despite ideological or economic differences.

Mexico is the product of an extensive racial and cultural mixture. As a result, we share in a variety of civilizations. Our independent life began 150 years ago during a period characterized by a world realignment of spheres of domination. For more than a century thereafter we lived through constant threats to our territory, foreign invasions, the loss of a large portion of our land and the systematic depletion of our resources. To a great extent, the history of our Republic is a reflection of the Mexican people's unflagging struggle to do away with the legacy of colonialism and to prevent outside interference in national affairs. Because of our origins and the difficult conditions in which we have developed, we are a country jealous of our own freedom and the freedom of all the peoples of the earth.

That is why the principles that invariably guide our foreign policy are the proscription of the use of force, the peaceful settlement of disputes, non-intervention, the juridical equality of States and the self-determination of peoples.

Our enthusiastic participation in the work of the United Nations from its inception, and our strict compliance with the commitments entered into within a spirit of loyal adherence to the ideals on which the Organization's existence rests, are not a mere coincidence.

I have come to this Assembly to reaffirm Mexico's adherence to the principles of the United Nations and to express its faith in the rapid advent of true international democracy, both political and economic.

The items on the agenda of this twenty-sixth session are particularly significant for the present and the future.

Mexico's recollection of its own War of Independence produces in our people a deep concern for the fate of the millions of human beings in different parts of the world who have not yet won their freedom.

Since 1945 we have favoured universality for our Organization; therefore our feeling of satisfaction at the constant growth of its membership from 51 to 130 nations—the most recently admitted States being Bhutan, Qatar and Bahrain—is easy to understand.

A noteworthy advance towards this principle of universality would be to welcome during this session the representatives of a nation inhabited by a fourth of the world's population—the People's Republic of China—and to give it its rightful place in the Security Council. At the same time, it will be necessary to recognize that the sovereignty and territorial integrity of the Chinese nation are juridically indivisible.

Disarmament, the absolute need to disarm—beginning with nuclear weapons—springs from peace as paramount among the values of human coexistence. Mexico has decisively contributed to work aimed at promoting disarmament at all the forums in which it has participated, and most particularly in the General Assembly and the Committee that specializes in this subject.

Furthermore, in the belief that one must practise what one preaches, we put forth our most determined efforts to complete successfully the task of banning atomic weapons in Latin America. The Tlatelolco Treaty was the culmination of this work. Thanks to this Latin American instrument, there is today an area of military denuclearization of 7 million square kilometers, comprising a population of approximately 120 million inhabitants. Our gratitude goes to U Thant, who, in his introduction to this year's report on the work of the Organization, appealed once again to all atomic powers to provide guarantees against nuclear violation of the area covered by the Treaty of Tlatelolco by signing and ratifying Additional Protocol II of that instrument, a justified appeal which my country also has been making and which I now reiterate most firmly.

The arms struggle that broke out in the Middle East in the spring of 1967 has given rise to a serious situation, the prompt settlement of which is incumbent not only on the parties directly affected by it, but also on all members of the international community since there is sound reason to believe that this conflict constitutes one of the most alarming threats of potential confrontation among the so-called Super-Powers. We continue to believe that resolution 242, adopted unanimously by the Security Council on November 22, 1967, is the right instrument to end this explosive conflict.

With respect to the serious situation posed by the presence of several million Pakistani refugees in India, Mexico requests the international community to make every effort to find a solution as quickly as possible that will allow these displaced persons to return to their homes.

The oceans that separate us geographically should unite us juridically. We should, therefore, strive to formulate a systematic, uniform, and equitable code in this field.

Perhaps the two most outstanding matters to be settled at the forthcoming conference on the law of the sea are the establishment of a system governing the sea-bed and the ocean floor, and the determination of the extent of territorial waters. The approach to the first of these should be on the basis of the 15 principles approved by the General Assembly last year, and particularly on the one which establishes that the sea-bed and the ocean floor are the common heritage of mankind.

We recognize the validity of the concern of several sister Latin American countries which claim maritime limits beyond 12 miles, on the grounds of their need to make use for their people of the resources that are becoming increasingly necessary for their subsistence, and in order to prevent their seizure by fishermen from distant lands. The time has come to define properly the special interest of coastal States in maintaining the productivity of the resources of the seas adjacent to their coasts and in the logical corollary of their sovereign right to establish exclusive and preferential fishing zones.

Environmental and development problems cannot be solved by the isolated action of any country, nor even by the joint action of a group of countries. A general mobilization is called for since, in the final analysis, what is being sought is the protection of the true protagonist of the drama we are witnessing—man himself.

Therefore, the importance of the United Nations Conference on the Human Environment to be held next year in Stockholm is unquestionable. Not only will the possibility of co-ordinating efforts come under study, but the point of departure will have to be the inescapable reality that most of the earth's surface and airspace are beyond the jurisdiction of nations, and for that reason their conservation demands international agreements.

Problems vary from region to region and even from city to city; solutions, therefore, must always be adapted to specific needs. Industrialization often produces polution, yet it is evident that no attempts should be made to hold back the development process. Any measure that hinders industrial progress in the weaker countries would be even less acceptable.

There has been a radical change in the political structure of the world in the last quarter of a century. The liberation of many nations that were under the yoke of colonialism has been accelerated, even though under the shadow of an armed peace in a time of uncertainty and fear.

It is my fond hope that this era of political "decolonialization" that we have been living in will be followed by another of economic "decolonialization" marked by shared progress among nations and by solidarity and effective action on their part in solving the problems that beset them.

The historical process which brought the benefits of modern civilization earlier to one group of nations caused an unbalanced stratification of the world community. The struggle for power among the industrialized countries went hand in hand with the advantages that accrued to them from their positions of dominance and the establishment of systems of exploitation that have survived into our times.

In the search for a new balance, we are now running the risk that shortsighted partisan interests will prevail over a more far-sighted willingness to cooperate. The only possible way of avoiding this danger is through reason, and this is its forum, the forum of truth.

United, the poor nations must establish the bases upon which they can share in the world community with dignity, and the limits beyond which they are not prepared to go; for them, international relations are not a matter of dominance but of independence and development. They repudiate all anachronistic power theories, and they hold that the independence of nations must lead them to the abandonment of oligarchic systems and the establishment of an international democratic society.

There will be no peace in the world until there has been a basic reorganization of economic relations among nations. Today, the threat of atomic war is as serious as that of the growing inequality between the rich countries and the poor.

Concepts of time and distance have been changed by means of communication, and peoples of all races and regions are at last learning the language of universal civilization. Thereby contrasts are sharpened, poverty is rendered more intolerable, the injustices of wars of aggression and the offences committed against international cooperation become more evident.

We must ponder the negative effects of allowing prejudices to continue in the form of disdain for peoples and cultures different from those of the powerful nations, and we must stop to reflect on the degree to which a lack of solidarity when it defies the patient work of the United Nations, may be considered a different expression of the same motives that lead to war.

One of the great virtues of the United Nations is that it has looked upon many peoples not as they were up to some years ago, but as what they can become in the future.

We must fight for the advent of an era of economic, social, and political equality, we must break the bonds of servitude, so that all peoples may fulfill their creative potentials at once. We must guide along peaceful paths just aspirations to freedom, health, food, housing, education, and full employment.

The demands of the majority of the world must not go unheeded. Our peoples are seeking answers and solutions to problems that have burdened them for many centuries, and they want to find them soon. The nature and the trend of the changes taking place over the face of vast continents depend in large measure on the attitude of the powerful nations towards those demands and on the efficacy of the machinery of cooperation.

Postwar hostilities are dissolving. At the same time, frustration and reaction against unfair treatment must be prevented from provoking a new and radical schism in the world between the affluent nations and those struggling to surmount underdevelopment.

However, no country or group of countries, however powerful they may be, may take upon themselves the exclusive guidance of world affairs, still less the guardianship of other nations.

We are now suffering from the negative consequences of systems that were not designed to satisfy, in the long run, the true needs of the international community.

A profound crisis is now manifest in the economic situation of the world—a crisis produced by defects in the regulatory machinery established at the end of World War II to reconcile the interests of the strongest countries and set up a financial system that was notoriously favourable to a dominant economy.

Widespread concern regarding underdevelopment was far from occupying a position of priority in the organizations responsible for ensuring peace. The chief concern was to rebuild the economies of the most highly developed countries, re-establishing international trends, and defining spheres of political influence.

The majority had no say in the decisions designed to create a world to suit the most powerful, and the turmoil we are now experiencing was brought on by substantial alterations in the relative economic levels of the rich countries.

Fortunately, solidarity among the developing nations now represents a political force in the formulation of new strategies. We know that the millions who make up the bulk of mankind are behind the principles set forth in the Latin American Consensus of Vina del Mar, the Charter of Tequendama, the Charter of Algiers, and General Assembly resolution 2626 (XXV).

The liberalization of world trade took years of arduous negotiation. We are relatively optimistic about the future after the adoption of the generalized system of preferences, despite the fact that the exemptions affected only tariff barriers and not the quantitative restrictions produced by import quotas.

The principle under which the industrialized nations grant tariff advantages to poorer ones to enable them to sell their manufactures competitively represents a step forward towards offsetting the existing imbalance among countries at varying stages of development. This is evident particularly if it is considered that the developing countres in fact grant tariff advantages on imports of products of the industrialized nations because they are unable to do without capital goods, machinery and equipment necessary for their progress.

Recently, we have been subjected to forces that obstruct the modest but positive results made to date.

It is a source of satisfaction to us that this General Assembly, when convening the third session of the United Nations Conference on Trade and Development (UNCTAD) should have expressed deep concern at the movement in certain countries towards the intensification of protectionism which damages the vital interests of the developing countries and stands in the way of the goals of the Second United Nations Development Decade.

I consider it my duty to point out that the levying of an additional 10% *ad valorem tax* on United States imports hurts my country's interests and those of all developing nations. A protectionist race must not come on the heels of an armaments race. We have already suffered from the effects of the transfer of the inflationary trends of the great powers, and now we are feeling the consequences of balance-of-payments deficits and internal unemployment.

The industrialized countries should bear in mind that temporary or permanent tariff barriers levied against poor countries are not only unjustified and unnecessary, but also self-defeating. Most of the developing countries already have a deficit in their balance of payments, which will now become more acute; their manufactures are just beginning to enter the markets of the industrialized nations and such measures will only force us to reduce our imports.

Furthermore, the developing world has been cooperating with the industrialized nations for many years by allowing them to invest in their countries and to obtain high profits, by becoming big customers for the industrialized nations' exports and suppliers of raw materials which they, in turn, process, enabling them thereby to trade anew with other economic powers.

Mexico reaffirms the principles set forth in the Manifesto of Latin America, which represents the unanimous consensus of the member nations of the Special Latin American Coordinating Committee vis-a-vis the situation brought about unilaterally by the United States on 15 August last.

It also reiterates its support of the theses which make up the International Development Strategy for the Second United Nations Dvelopment Decade containing most of the principles supported by the countries of the Group of 77, whose number has now grown considerably.

Special heed should be given to the opinions and needs of the developing countries in the reorganization of the international monetary system. The agreement of all is necessary to ensure its effectiveness; hence, there will be no problem in abiding by its rules. It should not be considered an instrument at the service of the most powerful economies, but rather as a factor for the expansion of economic activity to assure increasing flows of capital, on optimum terms and interest conditions, towards countries that need it.

Our country places special stress on the importance of the exchange of scientific and technological knowledge. For that reason it is closely watching the work of the Intergovernmental Group on Transfer of Technology. We feel sure the content of its report will contribute to the formulation of national and international policies to surmount the obstacles to public and multilateral action.

Although advances in the field of economic cooperation have not been spectacular and the serious obstacles I have referred to have indeed existed, there is no doubt that they have wrought a change in the principles upon which international trade theory was based. We trust that the next session of UNCTAD, to be held in Chile in 1972, will at last crystallize the main points upon which the hopes of the developing world rest.

While multilateral cooperation can be a factor for progress, the continuing growth of each country will be the outcome, primarily, of its own efforts and responsibility. Like all the countries of Latin America, Mexico is fighting against time to provide higher standards of living for its people.

Its goals concern mainly productivity and modernization of the agricultural economy, reorientation of industrial policy, redistribution of income, training of human resources, reorganization of public finances, and educational opportunities for all.

Economic integration is a collective instrument for accelerating the progress of Latin America. Its attainment should be one of the objectives of the national policy of all the countries of the area. Integration is an irreversible process, since our peoples already know that they cannot be left aside by trends towards the formation of larger economic areas. It is for this reason that Mexico is especially interested in having closer and more dynamic economic relations with all its neighbouring sister nations.

If this is to be achieved, it will be necessary to pay closer attention, among other mechanisms, to supplementary industrial agreements by the members of the Latin American Free Trade Association, to increase existing margins of preferences, to create truly Latin American multinational companies, to seek to replace our shortages of agricultural products with others of the region, and to improve regional financing machinery in order to facilitate the exporting of manufactures and semi-manufactures to third parties.

Mexico reasserts, on this occasion, its support for the Latin American integration process and expresses its eagerness to see this become a reality on a large scale.

There is nothing at the present time to justify great optimism with respect to the immediate future. At the same time, we find hope and encouragement in the knowledge that there are men of all races and ideologies who are giving the best of themselves to establish a just order. One of the most illustrious of these men is our Secretary-General, U Thant, who has devoted to the cause of peace his intelligence and determination together with his unlimited capacity to persuade and conciliate. As he has already announced, this will be the last session of the Assembly at which he will act in his distinguished post. Once again, on behalf of Mexico, at this time I wish to pay tribute to U Thant for the invaluable services he has rendered to the United Nations over the past decade.

With the succinctness the occasion demands, I have reviewed the items I believe to be of greatest importance among the many on our agenda. I offer these thoughts for the consideration of members of this Assembly. There can be no better repository for them than this forum, exponent *par excellence* of world opinion and the aspirations of the human race.

In taking my leave of you and expressing my appreciation for your kind willingness to hear me, I should like to conclude by reaffirming my faith and that of my people in the future of the United Nations. Our Organization is humanity's guide and mirror, and, therefore, our faith in the future runs parallel to our faith in man and his destiny.

The course of history is marked by advances and retreats, victories and defeats but, in the final analysis, there is always an irreversible gain. What has been attained domestically through the establishment of government by law must be achieved in the sphere of the international community we have all pledged to build. Its ideal structure is outlined in our Charter, each of its principles and aims represents a daily challenge that we must meet in a fitting manner.

OPPORTUNITIES FOR DEVELOPING NATIONS

Text of an address by Dr. Echeverria before the United Nations Conference on Trade and Development on April 19, 1972

Mexico reaffirms its faith in the high purpose of this conference. We firmly supported the United Nations initiative which summoned the member states to examine trade and development problems.

We thought we had found in the new interpretation of the international economy and the world's poverty problems a way of fulfilling the aspirations of our peoples, the presentation of which was entrusted to a celebrated Latin American. We saw in the world struggle for development the symbol of our time. We felt a new international order was being announced in which colonialism and dependence had no place. This was the historic encounter of mankind with its future.

Great expectations reigned in the first conference. The peripheral nations at that time were determined to obtain satisfaction for their just demands.

The industrial nations, for their part, seemed disposed to offer a more equitable treatment, in order to preserve in a different international setting the spheres of influence they had reserved.

The objectives aimed for then were those which peripheral nations deemed the essential minimum and were easily attainable. For primary commodities: stable prices and improved earnings. For manufactured goods: preferential access to markets and the elimination of non-tariff barriers. With regard to financing: transfers equivalent to one percent of the industrial nations' gross national product.

We are present at the third conference and most of these aspirations have yet to be realized. The developing countries have traveled the long road of frustration in the decade which spelled hope for mankind.

The principle of joint responsibility has not been honored. The adoption of satisfactory agreements is deferred to suit the convenience of one or more countries. Even worse, the decade has culminated with protectionist measures which provoke serious setbacks.

The terms of trade of important products have deteriorated: industrial nations are flooding the market with surplus goods; the transfer of financial resources has been reduced relative to the gross national product of the more advanced nations; and the developing nations which were intended to benefit from foreign lending find the foreign debt load hard to bear. The postponement of trade advantages already granted aggravates the imbalance in the balance of payments and generates dangerous repercussions in the political and social spheres.

The bipolar power structure and the prolonged struggles for supremacy relegate attention to the problems of peripheral nations to a secondary level. Colonial attitudes, which by now should have disappeared, still dominate international relations.

The centers of world power impose trade conditions upon the rest of the world. They also weaken the capacity of lesser developed countries for action, opposing essential structural changes or intervening in their political processes.

For the majority of our people, this has been a decade of increasing economic decline. There are more unemployed and illiterate people now than ten years ago. There is less job security and low wages are on the upswing. The surplus population which is not absorbed productively in the rural areas flocks to the cities and contributes to exacerbate the uneasy conditions caused by urban crowding. The concentration of wealth has increased and with respect to Latin America alone nearly half the inhabitants do not enjoy the fruits of development.

Population will double in the course of one generation. The productive apparatus must undergo a world-wide expansion in order to provide employment for the great marginal sectors and increase the well-being of those already employed.

We need to strengthen the responsibility of each village and each family with respect to the challenge which a high rate of population growth implies. It would be a mistake to accept without reservation urban attitudes which see in the population growth of marginal groups a threat to their own stability.

The rate of population growth must be reduced because it is expedient for our people: but the main task before us is to stimulate a vigorous and integrated development.

In the absence of an adequate framework of international cooperation our countries can hardly achieve a sufficiently accelerated economic growth to meet the social demands of a doubled population. On the other hand, the increasing deterioration of developing nations is the beginning of a process of involution which affects all mankind.

The progress of mankind as of this moment is indivisible. Events in each country affect all the others and condition their evolution. To view the future in purely local terms is to ignore the international character of the present-day economy. No community can fully resolve its problems without considering them from a general perspective.

This is not just a confrontation between the rich and the dispossessed nations of the world. The interests of advanced and developing nations can and must converge. We must realize that responsibilities must be shared in the world of today and the future.

We are present at this meeting because we believe that, in spite of the meagre results obtained, the philosophy and methods proposed by UNCTAD—today more than ever—represent the only viable alternative for progress and survival. Only the generalized participation of all the nations in world trade can break the stranglehold on today's economy and avoid a new era of social upheaval.

The last five years were characterized by an unprecedented expansion in world trade. Nevertheless the increase in the volume of transactions has primarily favored the most prosperous nations and has left only meagre benefits to developing nations. Thus, in spite of our objectives, trade has widened the gap between nations.

The recent protectionist measures and the monetary crisis itself confirm this tendency. To put aside the problems of productivity and employment originating in industrial societies is to turn one's back on the world of poverty and confine oneself to an increasingly artificial competition between the developed nations.

To accumulate riches where there already is abundance is self-defeating. The powerful nations could initiate a healthier process of growth and full employment if they widened the scope of their transactions.

The more advanced economies will not consolidate their gains without increasing their trade with underdeveloped nations. The latter for their part cannot undergo change without acquiring through increasing exports the necessary capital and technology for development.

By recognizing the economic inequality between nations and acting to reduce it we reaffirm the principle of legal equality between nations.

The future of this organization would be in considerable danger if we were unable to put into practice the general system of preferences which in lengthy negotiations obtained the approval of all nations.

To facilitate the export of manufactured goods from countries which are in the process of industrialization is an effective stimulus in promoting the evolution of their economic and social structures. Such action presupposes a new concept of the international division of labor which does not stem from the so-called natural order of things, but is a means of obtaining the integral development of all nations.

We must be wary of neocolonial attitudes shrouded in so-called scientific theories which tend to limit the industrial progress of our peoples. Such reasoning in the economic sphere reveals the same prejudices and interests as racism with respect to human relations.

It is obvious that the economic future of our people does not depend on immutable factors or on an imaginary determinism but on their ability to adapt modern technology to their natural resources and to the labor of their inhabitants.

A real era of international economic cooperation must be born. The general and non-discriminatory character of the preferential system has a profound political content. On the one hand, it exceeds the bounds of the great powers' spheres of influence, and on the other it confirms the multilateral character of the action undertaken by UNCTAD.

The solutions developed by this Conference do not diminish but strengthen the power of self-determination. Their implicit purpose is not to compromise or loan out the sovereignty of the member states. We strive for an interdependent economy based on equity not on conditions.

There are indications that some highly developed capitalist nations which have not offered preferences propose to defer meeting their obligations on that score. If this is true, we run the risk of annulling the decision of nations which have already set the system into operation.

The industrial socialist nations have also decided to grant preferences to developing nations. Nevertheless, some of them have not yet presented the concrete outlines of the benefits they propose to offer. These nations usually support the demand of Third World nations, but in practice their attitude has not been translated into a significant opening of their markets or an appreciable flow of capital or technical resources.

Our nations view with disappointment the fact that the atmosphere of international forums is filled with words that are rarely followed by actions. It is essential that resolutions binding on all parties emerge from this Conference. It is useless for us to waste our time asking for what others are unwilling to give, in reaching precarious agreements and feeling sorry later because such promises are broken.

Nevertheless, UNCTAD would fail if it were to become only a forum for recrimination. We conceive it as an instrument for negotiation and we are determined to strengthen it. The respect of all states for the agreements made at this Conference and in fulfillment of freely accepted terms will bear witness henceforward to the degree of maturity attained by the community of nations.

The developed nations with a market economy have announced that they intend to undertake in 1973 new negotiations within the framework of the General Agreement on Tariffs and Trade. Our nations should not be excluded once more from the expansion of world trade.

To that end, this Conference, as the Latin American nations have decided, must establish instruments which guarantee the participation of all developing nations in these negotiations whether they are members of said agreement or not.

To the many difficulties limiting the growth of the less developed nations we must add the effect of inflationary pressures from abroad. Developing nations bitterly resent the effects of a monetary crisis which they did nothing to provoke. Nevertheless, they have not been consulted in the search for possible solutions.

Economic inequality is reflected in the voting power of nations within the international financing organizations. It is necessary to increase the participation of developing nations in the decision-making process of the International Monetary Fund, thereby making it a more democratic institution.

It is essential to restructure and strengthen the International Monetary Fund as well as the International Bank for Reconstruction and Development. This institution, having repaired the effects of a conflict which took place more than a quarter of a century ago, must dedicate its future efforts exclusively to development and therefore support only developing countries.

International financing should never be subject to political considerations. It defies reason moreover to deny it to nations which try revolutionary methods in their search for progress.

The monetary order being developed must be subject to the objectives of the international development strategy. Postwar reconstruction proved the efficacy of economic international cooperation. At this time a second massive transfer of resources must be undertaken directed towards the peripheral nations to correct the many distortions in the contemporary economy and open the way towards a prosperity shared by all nations.

We support the idea of establishing a link between the granting of special drawing rights and additional financing for development. We propose that the high degree of liquidity of world financial markets be used for the same purpose. There are real possibilities for channelling resources towards less developed countries at a greater rate than the one percent established by this Conference.

Excellent opportunities will arise to channel supplementary resources in the immediate future to developing nations. A treaty is in the process of being signed which prohibits the manufacture, possession and transfer of biological weapons and orders the destruction of existing stockpiles, a document to which Mexico fully adheres.

Imitative attitudes and deliberate influences often arrest the capitalization of poor nations. The premature adoption of styles of consumption and methods of production which reduce investment capabilities and create unemployment is not development but fictional progress.

Direct foreign investments that do not share responsibility with national entrepreneurs, or provide for the transfer of technological innovations and a corresponding access to the benefits derived from foreign markets, are only an extension of the old forms of colonialism. In any case, they must be subject to the laws and development objectives of the host nations.

Multinational corporations can contribute significantly to the modernization of our economies. Their cumulative technological capability would permit them to avoid the old systems of exploitation of human and material resources characteristic of oil and mining companies, which left such a bitter aftermath in our countries.

We need to increase our nations' capacity to create, assimilate and adapt the technology which is now concentrated predominantly in the industrial nations. The latter must collaborate to finance research programs and promote the establishment of highly specialized centers to face our specific problems of productivity and employment.

For the first time in the history of UNCTAD, the agenda includes the study of a report by a working group made on the specific problems of the transfer of technology. We hope that a special commission on this issue emerges from these deliberations. Mexico would firmly support such action.

This Conference should stimulate the establishment of adequate institutions to act as outlets for the transfer of technology, licensing banks and technological information centers to which developing countries might turn for assistance.

Every nation must recognize and honor the right of every other to dispose freely of its natural resources without any outside pressure or interference. For their part multinational corporations must abstain from intervening directly or indirectly in matters which pertain only to the sovereign decision-making process of each nation.

The optimum use of maritime resources has become the imperative of our age. Immoderate and irrational exploitation endangers many species, which are close to extinction. The activity of foreign fishermen in the coastal waters of developing nations unjustifiably limits their economic advancement and provokes constant international friction.

Mexico sympathizes with its sister nations' efforts to avoid serious conflict yet to remain firm in their determination to establish a 200-mile territorial sea.

Without impairing these aspirations, Mexico will strive in the World Conference of the Law of the Sea in 1973 to obtain the legal recognition of a patrimonial sea extending 200 miles off shore, in which the coastal state would unquestionably exercise exclusive and preferential fishing rights over all economic resources.

Aside from the legal aspect, the improved utilization of maritime resources is an economic problem which primarily concerns UNCTAD. The subject is of paramount interest to developing countries, not only because maritime resources provide high protein food with which to feed their increasing populations, but because the exploitation of resources can be a powerful instrument in their economic development.

The progressive deterioration of the environment affects the whole of humanity. On the other hand, there is a strong link between environmental problems and industrial progress. Nevertheless, the issue of pollution must not be translated into measures which place obstacles in the peripheral nations' desire for economic progress.

Similarly it is the fundamental duty of the more industrial nations to adopt the necessary research and economic policies to correct the present situation for which they are primarily responsible.

The complex structure of the international economy has witnessed the rise of nations which have attained intermediate levels of advancement. It would be unjust for them to monopolize all the benefits of economic cooperation, giving weaker nations the same treatment which they themselves received from the great powers in the past. Let us not commit the same historic error incurred by the great powers.

Solidarity is a test successful men and communities often fail. To be equitable means to grant special privileges to nations which in an unbalanced world receive the most unjust treatment.

Mexico will favor the adoption of concrete measures in support of the relatively less developed countries. Within our capability we will grant special treatment without demanding reciprocity to Latin American countries recognized as such by our regional organizations.

We do not believe, however, that underdeveloped countries must carry the load of the less developed countries among them. The issue is to transfer by means of trade, financing and technology the necessary resources from centers of greater economic power to those which have had less access to the benefits of the modern economy.

Economic regional integration is an ideal method for accelerating development and an irreversible process which tends to form wider economic units. It multiplies the possibilities of trade and provides higher levels of industrialization. It also widens the scope for negotiation and therefore strengthens the fulfillment of the Conference's objectives.

A free-trade zone in Latin America opens the way towards closer economic, cultural, technological and political ties. At this time I repeat my faith in the Latin American process of integration and the sympathy with which Mexico views similar attempts in Africa and Asia which tend to unify the efforts of Third World nations.

We propose that the so-called Group of 77 be considered an established association without prejudice to the importance and integrity of the present forum. We firmly believe that there are no fundamental differences between countries which expect common answers to similar problems. Such unity would be more easily attained if a single forum of free debate and a permanent working site not subject to the time frame imposed by higher authorities were available.

We must strengthen the precarious legal bases of the international economy. A just order and a stable world are not possible as long as there are no rights and duties to protect weak nations. Let us separate economic cooperation from the sphere of good will and transfer it to the field of law. Let us apply the principles of solidarity among men to the conduct of relations between nations.

Throughout the years the bases for a possible Charter of Economic Rights and Duties of States to complement the Universal Declaration of Human Rights have emerged.

The recognition by the community of nations of the just demands of our peoples permit us to outline some of these principles:

i) Freedom [for each nation] to dispose at will of its natural resources.

ii) Respect for each nation's absolute right to adopt the economic structure which it deems most suitable and to impose upon private property the requirements the public interest dictates.

iii) Renunciation of methods and instruments of economic pressure which reduce the political sovereignty of nations.

iv) Subordination of foreign capital to the laws of the host nation.

v) Express prohibition against intervention in the internal affairs of nations by multinational corporations.

vi) Abolition of commercial practices which discriminate against the exports of non-industrial nations.

vii) Economic preferences proportional with the level of development.

viii) Agreements which guarantee the stability and fair price of primary commodities.

ix) Ample and adequate transfer of scientific and technological advances at the lowest cost and as rapidly as possible to the most underdeveloped nations.

x) Allocation of greater resources to long-term development financing with no conditions attached and at low interest rates.

The solidarity we request is a matter of survival. If developing nations were to be neglected once more in the process of adjustment which they are now experiencing, the world powers would be further divided economically and the relative international stability we have attained would not last long.

Short-term solutions, though apparently correct, are often proved historically wrong. A truly effective solution rises above circumstantial interests and confronts the future fairly and squarely.

Peace is not only disturbed by weapons. Let us prepare for the 21st century by understanding that there is but a single future for mankind. History is on our side because our view of the world envisions an effective possibility of peace and prosperity.

This is the task for the present generation and it cannot be postponed any longer. We are on the threshhold of a structural change in human society which will only take place if all nations participate in the endeavour.

If the experience of the past decade repeats itself in this one, the damage done to the relations between Third World and industrial nations will be perhaps irreparable.

A balance cannot be achieved as long as the agreement of the majority of the inhabitants of the world is not obtained. Our people are aware that their poverty is used to provide other peoples' wealth. The resentment aroused by political colonialism is now turned against economic colonialism.

It is the main duty of the international community to build an economy for peace. On the other hand, refusal to cooperate in order to reduce the differences between nations is to avoid fulfilling the principles of the United Nations.

Perhaps the era of international conferences will also end if we prove incapable of finding the formula for a balanced development, just as the era of unproductive negotiations also ended on the eve of the world wars. Our debates will only remain as testimony of our indignation and inabilty to understand and once more history will bear the imprint of irrationality.

We make an urgent appeal to those who decisively influence the conduct of the economy of the world and likewise to the representatives of the nations which have the most to gain from our deliberations. Our appeal is made with the certainty that civility in the time of crisis is the only unifying course in the service of hope. The task of our time is to convert all the tumult of dissatisfaction into an organized force for progress and freedom.

The political will of 141 nations is a force with a strength equal to the problems we face. We must continue our efforts in the calm spirit of negotiation.

I thank the members of this Conference and in particular its Secretary-General, who have bestowed on me the honor of expressing before this historic assembly the attitude of my country on issues which concern the international community.